GRADUATION FROM A SHAOLIN TEMPLE WAS DIFFICULT . . .

A student must pass three tests.

The first was a difficult oral examination on the art's history, theory and significant thought.

Then came the harrowing ordeal. The student had to work his way through a booby-trapped hallway. One hundred eight wooden dummies with spears, knives and clubs attacked him as he triggered a mechanical device under the floor with his own weight.

Next, his way was blocked by a five-hundred pound smoldering urn that he must lift with his forearms, burning into his flesh two sculpted symbols of a tiger and dragon.

Now, he was branded—and free. And wherever he travelled, he would be an honored, respected Shaolin monk.

The Wisdom of
KUNG FU

by Michael Minick

**WARNER
PAPERBACK
LIBRARY**

A Warner Communications Company

WARNER PAPERBACK LIBRARY EDITION
First Printing: August, 1975

Copyright © 1974 by Michael Minick

Grateful acknowledgment is hereby made to the Prints Division,
New York Public Library, Astor, Lenox and Tilden Foundations, for
use of the illustrations that appear in this book.

Grateful acknowledgment is made to reprint excerpts from THE
WISDOM OF CHINA AND INDIA, edited by Lin Yutang.
Copyright 1942 and renewed 1970 by Random House, Inc. Re-
printed by permission of the publisher.

Library of Congress Catalog Card Number: 74-6257

This Warner Paperback Library Edition is published by
arrangement with William Morrow and Company, Inc.

Warner Paperback Library is a division of Warner Books, Inc.,
75 Rockefeller Plaza, New York, N.Y. 10019.

Cover design by Gene Light

Book design by Milton Batalion

Cover photograph by Neil Slavin

Ⓦ A Warner Communications Company

Printed in the United States of America

Not associated with Warner Press, Inc. of Anderson Indiana

This book is dedicated to Robert M. Heller . . . a man who knows the true meanings of friendship. His patience, belief, and understanding led to my first job in publishing. At every point in my career he was there to help and advise me, and this book is no exception. Not only did he introduce me to the man who became my literary agent (Jay Sanford), but he even supplied the initial idea from which this book grew.

Contents

視聽自民圖

PART 1

1
What Is Kung Fu?

Real kung fu, as differentiated from the media variety, is something very special, and as such is not readily defined nor labeled. Real kung fu is a spirit, an idea, a folk culture, a way of living. Rendering its essence into words is like describing the moon to a blind man.

If, for the moment, kung fu could be reduced to its least common denominator it would be as the public sees it—a form of self-defense. And while personal combat is indeed a significant segment of the art, kung fu outgrew these narrow confines thousands of years ago. Traditionally, kung fu men and women (while China has a long sexist tradition, kung fu does not; top masters and warriors were frequently women) were expected to study the wisdom and skills of a wide variety of professions including scholarship, alchemy, weaponry, practical philosophy (i.e., Taoism and Buddhism), and Chinese medicine. Students who were able to master all these diverse fields were called *sifu* or master. Many masters were frequently priests, monks, nuns, or hermits as only they had the leisure time to study all the required skills. Consequently, masters were always rare and particularly so in this day and age. Much more common were kung fu men or women who had achieved some skill in one or more of the above areas. (To avoid confusion and repetition, men and women who practice the art will be referred to as kung fu men.) It soon becomes apparent that western culture possesses nothing that is even remotely similar to kung fu. To further explain this, enigmatic art—and any means of self-defense practiced by religious orders is very mysterious—it is necessary to fall back on the tool of comparison.

The closest thing to kung fu is another eastern discipline—yoga. The similarities are so overwhelming that if the martial aspect of kung fu is disregarded, the art could be called Chinese yoga. Both systems possess a form of medical gymnastics whose purpose isn't just to build bulging muscles, but to develop stronger internal organs. Herbal remedies are an important part of the training of the yogi and kung fu man. Deep breathing and meditational exercises play a vital role in both approaches, and many of the techniques are identical. In addition, there are some schools of kung fu and yoga that practice these techniques solely, to the exclusion of other disciplines. Yoga, like kung fu, is not a religion; thus it encourages its student to study spiritual thought and literature. As both methods are interested in Buddhism, the same texts are frequently used.

Both methods recognize the importance of dietary control and have similar programs. The highest goal of each approach is the same—tuning into one's mysterious inner energy (called *prana* in yoga, and *chi* in kung fu). Masters of both schools are able to use this energy to accomplish incredible feats. Lying on a bed of knives, being buried alive for days, are simple chores for those skilled in tapping their internal powers.

Monasteries, traditionally the training grounds for yogis, have also enjoyed wide use in kung fu. And one of the most important figures in kung fu history, Ta Mo, was himself a yogi. An Indian patriarch, best known for bringing Zen Buddhism to China, he also introduced a series of health exercises that later evolved into one of the most influential branches of kung fu. In the final analysis, yoga and kung fu are similar because they both represent methods of gaining total control over the workings of the mind and body.

Exercises, meditation, monasteries, self-defense are all tools which the master ultimately discards when true wisdom is gained. Thus it is said that a true master no longer needs to practice exercises or self-defense forms, but simply sits down and performs the exercises mentally to achieve the same results. For the advanced student, kung fu or yoga becomes a way of *thinking* that permits the individual to transcend common worldly cares, fear, and frustrations, to live life in a state of peaceful harmony.

Perhaps nothing reflects the true spirit of kung fu as much as the words themselves. Rendered into English, kung fu means a discipline that requires considerable time and work to master. Consequently, anyone who has spent years learning or mastering a skill is described as "learned or possessed of kung fu." Since all Chinese ideograms have several meanings, kung fu is sometimes referred to as: a task, a piece of work that is to be accomplished, an accumulation of time and work, a generic name for exercise, or any achievement in scholarship or learning of any kind. The overall wisdom implications of the word are further magnified by the fact that the name of Confucius, the revered philosopher, in Chinese is Kung Fu Tzu. An additional meaning that reflects another facet of the art is "fire and time." Used in relation to alchemy, which many early kung fu men practiced, it denotes the correct time an alchemist would keep a fire burning to concoct a drug or panacea.

Ironically, what the West knows as kung fu is not called kung fu among the Chinese. In the Orient the proper word is wu su, which translates as national arts or martial arts. (For the sake of convenience and familiarity kung fu will be the term used throughout this book.) The proper name no doubt refers to the root from which kung fu sprang—self-defense. This is as it should be, because kung fu as it was originally formulated only encompassed four areas: wrestling, weaponry, pugilism, and health nourishment. It took thousands of years before other disciplines were added to the list of required skills. Thus many masters here and abroad, recognizing the inadequacy of the traditional name, called their art kung fu/wu su—meaning an accumulation of knowledge and physical skill that may be used as a means of self-defense.

How wu su came to be known as kung fu in the West is another story. Since it took an enormous amount of time to master wu su it became commonplace in certain Chinese provinces to refer to such an expert as one possessed of kung fu. For similar reasons, Chinese people in western countries began calling the *art* kung fu rather than the individual man. In time, both the art and the man became one in the public's eye. Ironically, what began as a colloquial expression usurped the meaning of the original term.

THE KUNG FU HERO

Perhaps the heart and soul of the art are best summed up in the lives and exploits of the kung fu hero. Possessing seemingly superhuman abilities, he was the traditional protector of the weak and oppressed in Chinese culture. Robin-Hood style, he took from the rich to aid the poor. Roughly a cross between a knight in armor, wild West gunslinger, and a Taoist sage, he captured the imagination of Chinese everywhere. Required to take an oath, pledging to aid the helpless and punish evildoers, he has been emulated by Chinese youth for centuries. Even today countless numbers flock to kung fu parlors in the hopes of mastering the intricacies of the art. Those seeking instruction are still required to sign an oath of allegiance, promising to use the techniques taught to them for honorable purposes.

Of course good intentions and a pledge are seldom sufficient tools to help someone in trouble—these needed to be backed up by a high degree of skill. Thus any true master, who was a credit to his teacher, was capable of simultaneously dispatching two, three, four, or more assailants. And he was expected to accomplish this with one of the numerous strange and difficult Chinese weapons, or else, with his bare hands. Well versed in military tactics, he was particularly adept at leading his enemies into deadly traps. Toward this end, many enterprising masters developed smokes and powders to blind their attackers or knock them unconscious, making kung fu men the first to utilize chemical warfare. In addition to mastering weapons, they also created them. Ingenious mechanical devices, the world's first booby traps and hidden weapons, were part of the kung fu hero's arsenal against evildoers. Probably the most potent weapon the kung fu masters possessed was their *chi*, or inner energy. Through years of practice and meditation, a true master could perform incredible feats of strength and endurance. Documented cases of ordinary people who have lifted cars and pianos to save a loved one pinned beneath are well known throughout the western world. A kung fu master, after years of hard work, could perform this type of feat and even more astounding acts at will. Against that type of ability few thugs had a chance.

Of course, the ability to take someone apart is not enough to make a man a hero—he must also be able to put a man back together again. And since sparring practice or actual combat produced a wide range of injuries it became necessary to learn traditional Chinese medicine. Initially emphasis was placed on ointments and baths that toughened the body, as well as basic skills like setting broken bones and caring for open wounds. Time broadened this basic knowledge as many realized that as a fighter, a kung fu man was only as strong as his health. As a result, emphasis was placed on an overall approach to medicine. Preventive medicine took on greater importance, particularly exercise systems that were designed to keep the internal functions of the body working smoothly. Acupuncture points, originally taught as a weapon because of their capacity to cripple, were learned with an eye toward keeping the body strong and treating disease. Herbal preparations used to strengthen external weaknesses became a daily item in the kung fu man's diet. After classes, masters frequently served their students hot herbal drinks to clear up any possible internal congestion that resulted from the rigorous training they endured. All these skills taken together produced a remarkable health program that was second to none throughout China and possibly the rest of the world. Naturally such medical abilities made the kung fu hero a welcome and respected guest wherever he traveled, spreading the legend and esteem of his art throughout his homeland.

Yet, the kung fu hero was not considered complete unless he was also a man of letters and refinement. Much of his rigorous training was directed toward scholarship. He was expected to be well versed in the thoughts and sayings of China's great poets, philosophers, and sages. This was no simple trick considering the vast number of books and philosophies that existed in ancient China. Moreover, using this knowledge he was expected to be able to compose tricky multimeaning poems, puns, and repartees in verse, upon request. As good guitars were as much the companion of kung fu heroes as good swords, some sort of musical training was equally important. A man who did not possess at least some musical ability was considered to be a man out of touch with his soul. In much the same vein, calligraphy, elevated to an art in China, was widely considered a mirror of the true man. And a kung fu hero's hand had to pass the scrutiny of the world's first handwriting analysts in order to demonstrate that he was the cultured man he represented himself to be.

Finally, despite his martial training, the kung fu man was expected to be a man of peace. Usually a Taoist or Buddhist, he declined violence unless it was a last resort. As a man on the path of spiritual enlightenment his principal concern was to achieve a tranquil nature by gaining complete control of his mind and body. Thus wisdom and kindness took precedence over worldly concern. To such a man material wealth and fame were fleeting pleasures, whose impact was quickly dissipated like a wave breaking on the shore. The kung fu hero strove to know the real meanings of things and turned inward for the answers. This Buddha-like nature was highly regarded among his contemporaries, and perhaps it was this more than his other skills that placed him so far above ordinary men.

As a result Chinese fascination with the kung fu hero was something of a national obsession until the Communist takeover in 1950 when he was replaced by the proletariat hero of the new regime. This fascination is still evident in Taiwan and Hong Kong where kung fu books and periodicals are published at an enormous rate. Unfortunately, the grain of violence in these stories runs a bit deep nowadays, distorting the very principles that made the kung fu hero the revered figure he was in the not-too-distant past. But then it was violence itself that created the kung fu hero, and Chinese history is filled with violent epochs that alternate with periods of relative stability.

Until recent history, China was a feudal society akin to that of medieval Europe. It was a culture frequently governed by regional warlords (a word that is of Chinese origin), similar to European barons who employed armored knights to defend their peasants and property. The sole difference was that in China kung fu experts replaced hired knights. Predictably this wild environment gave birth to another kind of kung fu man—the criminal. While most people learn the ancient arts for decent and humanitarian reasons, there have always been a number who have sought knowledge for corrupt and evil purposes. Thus the renegade is as much a part of kung fu as is the hero.

In other eras, these bandits took advantage of the lawless times to loot and pillage the countryside at will. Renegade experts formed schools for crime. There they trained large numbers of outlaws in the martial arts and molded them into well-disciplined gangs. Many of the warlords of the era were themselves no better than criminals, terrorizing the peasants until they lived little better than slaves. Gangs controlled large territories and virtually ran important towns. Still others took over Buddhist or Taoist temples—either killing the monks or making them their servants—as they usurped the temples for their headquarters and training grounds. This sacrilegious use of temples was carried out with an eye toward defense, as many of the temples were secure and easily defendable from attacks by other gangs and occasional government troops.

Even in the twentieth century there have been many cases where kung fu schools have housed little more than street gangs, at continual war with other schools and systems. Hong Kong, until recently, was plagued by this type of strife where masters issued open challenges to any school to match styles. School signs were torn down (a grave insult) and some gangs, after vicious melees, took over a rival's systems hall! Fortunately, this was brought to an end, as the different schools realized that they were hurting the art.

Today, kung fu is enjoying a much-needed revival. A new spirit of cooperation in evident, and the old values are once again flourishing. The same schools that were fighting each other in Hong Kong have now joined efforts and formed an association to resolve differences and promote the art. Even in Communist China, kung fu has undergone a revival. The government has gone to considerable expense and trouble to initiate interest in the art, although with a revolutionary slant. Under its aegis obscure forms have been studied and preserved. And to see that the public benefits from these efforts, Communist presses turn out dozens of books on various aspects of the art. Where secrecy once prevailed, masters everywhere are sharing their knowledge with others. And ultimately, it is knowledge that kung fu is all about.

2

The History of Kung Fu

Tracing the development of kung fu is a tricky undertaking. The true history of the art is obscured by countless legends, texts of doubtful authenticity, and a veil of secrecy the kung fu masters themselves have drawn over the art. The reason behind this secrecy goes back to the time when open competition between masters was commonplace. This allowed unscrupulous masters to study surreptitiously the tactics of others in order to devise a defense for an actual battle. As many of these challenges were fought to the death, this type of martial-art espionage led to the withdrawal of individual kung fu styles from the public eye and the eventual withdrawal of kung fu itself. Consequently, kung fu suffered a decline in prestige and popular support. It is only since the latter part of the twentieth century that different schools are emerging into the open. A direct result of this isolation is that each school has a different legend about the beginnings of kung fu. Yet, from the many tales available, there are a number of reasonably solid facts that most schools agree upon.

It is known that the first reported forms of kung fu are almost five thousand years old. Reputedly, the

葛伯仇餉圖

great Yellow Emperor, Huang Ti, used an early form of the art with startling success in an important battle in roughly 2674 B.C. Records indicate that this rudimentary kung fu, then called chiou ti, was both a military tactic as well as a form of individual combat. The general consensus is that this style of kung fu may have been restricted to weapon techniques.

In approximately 2600 B.C. a form of wrestling and hand-to-hand combat developed that many experts believe was the most original form of kung fu. Called go-ti, this bloody "sport" was supposedly invented by an evil warlord named Chi-yu who was finally defeated by Hsien-yuan Wangti in the battle of Tuluk. But before his demise Chi-yu invented a sadistic game in which his soldiers were forced to fight each other with helmets that sported two long sharp horns. The object of the game was to gore the opponent; hence the name go-ti, which means horn gore. To escape being gored called for some pretty fancy footwork, which in turn resulted in the beginnings of unarmed self-defense. In time, the sport was modified and the horns removed. Civilians began to practice go-ti and the tradition was handed down from generation to generation. While go-ti as originally formulated is no longer practiced today, during festivals the natives of Honan, Manchuria, and Shanshi still entertain themselves with an ancient go-ti dance that simulates the original form of combat.

Meanwhile another equally interesting development was taking place. Scholar-monks in the fifth century A.D. have described an ancient series of medical gymnastics called cong fu. Reputedly practiced prior to 2600 B.C., these exercises combined specific physical movements and postures with breathing techniques to keep the body healthy, the mind alert, and the spirit tranquil. The existence of these exercises has been further corroborated by certain legends in Chinese medical history. During the same era, Huang Ti, the Yellow Emperor, nationalized the art of medicine by appointing medical agents and sending them throughout the empire to prescribe the proper treatments for common illnesses, including medical gymnastics to maintain health. No doubt these exercises marked the beginning of what the fifth century scholar-monks called cong fu and is most likely the first recorded account of the use of kung fu for medicinal purposes.

Meanwhile, the martial side of kung fu continued to develop and gain considerable importance in everyday life. During the turbulent seventh and eighth centuries B.C. it was recorded in the *Book of Songs (Shih Ching)* that: "Without boxing techniques, a man is relegated to the lower ranks of the army." This was particularly significant to the average man who was expected to serve for two years in the military service between the ages of twenty-three and fifty-six. But it was in the sixth century B.C. that was to totally change the direction of kung fu and elevate it from the realm of mere self-defense.

The first event of importance early in the sixth century was the pronouncement of Confucius on the necessity of cultivating the martial arts. Best known as the sage whose philosophy molded Chinese culture for thousands of years, Confucius was undoubtedly familiar with early forms of kung fu. Many authorities believe that his students were also required to learn secret unarmed combat techniques. In his writing he said: "As there are literary arts, there should be military arts." Thus he included archery and charioteering in the six arts that he taught his disciples. The other four—writing, mathematics, music, and propriety —reflect the many abilities the kung fu hero of a later era was expected to possess.

Even more significant were the teachings of the great sage Lao Tzu. Living at the same time as Confucius, Lao Tzu wrote the *Tao-te Ching (The Power and the Way)* which sets forth the wisdom of Taoism in beautiful poetic passages. Essentially a philosophic system rather than a religious one, Taoism is a way of achieving higher states of consciousness, not unlike yoga and similar disciplines. Lao Tzu's wisdom was rapidly incorporated into the developing schools of kung fu and from this point on the two disciplines grew side by side, and at times meshed completely. Both schools developed into systems which encompassed breath control, meditation techniques, physical exercises, medical practices, alchemy, and scholarship. Taoist monks became kung fu experts in all forms of combat, although they were particularly recognized for their special proficiency with swords and other weapons. In turn, kung fu men took to heart Taoist ways and lived their lives by the dicta of that philosophy. Although there is no way to know for sure, it is assumed that this era saw the formulation of the kung fu code which called for the protection of the weak and punishment of evildoers.

During the Han Dynasty kung fu and its companion art go-ti became increasingly popular and for the first time in history truly caught the public fancy. Credit for this widespread popularity is commonly attributed to the reign of the emperor Han Wu Ti (157-87 B.C.) who was himself an ardent student and promoter of the sport. This new and widespread interest was reflected in the historical annals of the dynasty. The *Book of Han*, written almost two hundred years after Han Wu Ti's reign, hails the new importance of the art. Pan Ku, its author, devotes four chapters to kung fu strategy dealing with: configuration, positive and negative principles in nature, Machiavellianism, and skill. The skill chapter alone is 199 pages long and deals in considerable detail with hand-to-hand combat, fencing, exercises utilizing the arms and legs, the use of a wide variety of weapons, and ways to lead an enemy into a trap.

Chinese medicine supplied the next significant advancement of the art. Written records describe a brilliant doctor named Hua T'o (A.D. 190-265) who devised a sequence of movements to relieve muscular and emotional tension while tonifying the body. While medical gymnastics had been popular for years, Hua T'o's exercises are of considerable importance in that they were based upon the movements of different animals—a pattern that more advanced kung fu forms would follow a thousand years later! Hua, consistently ahead of his time, is also credited with the discovery of anesthetics, which he concocted by mixing various herbs with wine. One of his lectures, which appears in the *Hou Han-Shu Chronicles*, convincingly puts forth his views and seems as though it could have been written by a later-day kung fu master. "The body needs exercise," he explains, "but not to the point of exhaustion, for exercise expels the bad air from the system, promotes the free circulation of blood and prevents sickness. The used doorstep never rots, so it is with the body. I have a system of exercises called 'The Frolics of the Five Animals.' The movements are those of tiger, deer, bear, monkey, and bird. This system removes disease, strengthens the legs [considered essential in kung fu], and insures health. It consists of jumping, twisting, swaying, crawling, rotating, and contracting."

Kung fu continued to flourish, and sometime during the Hou Han era (A.D. 25-220) the first modern style was developed. Originated by Kwok Yee, and known as the "Long Hand" style, this method was designed to subdue opponents from a longer range than hand-to-hand combat. This was of particular importance as most techniques of the period only worked at close range. Long hand rapidly became the predominant defensive form and enjoyed considerable refinement. Masters became so skilled in this style that Emperor Niwanti (A.D. 535-551) in his book *Classic Literature*, wrote that the long hand technique enabled a practitioner to defeat heavily armed opponents with his bare hands!

The next major influence on the art came in roughly A.D. 520 with the arrival of the Buddhist monk Ta Mo from India. Ta Mo was the twenty-eighth patriarch after Gautama, the original buddha. Accounts of why he came to China conflict. Some say he was captured during a military expedition; others insist he wished to bring Buddhism to the Chinese. Whatever the reason, he was presented to the emperor and allowed to retire to the Shaolin Temple. Legend tells us that his predominant activity during his first nine years in China was to face a wall and meditate until he was so in tune with the environment that he could discern the movements of insects behind him! Ta Mo's subsequent contributions were equally extraordinary. Although he translated many Buddhist texts, he is particularly remembered for his Chinese interpretation of Buddhism known as Ch'an or Zen Buddhism. This method eventually gained enormous popularity, momentarily eclipsing other schools of spiritual thought. As a result, Ta Mo became the first Chinese patriarch and is honored throughout China with the title Bodhidharma.

True Buddhism, like Taoism, is not another religion, but a mental discipline and a way of thought that is akin to yoga. The impact of Buddhism or kung fu was every bit as profound as Taoism one thousand years earlier. The mystical concept of the "empty mind," the koan (an enigmatic unanswerable riddle meant to bring spiritual awareness in a flash of intuitive cognition), and other forms of Zen-style meditation were rapidly incorporated into the art. As Buddhism is firmly grounded in peace and nonviolence, it further strengthened and fortified the kung fu code.

On the physical level, one of the most vital aspects of Ta Mo's legacy are his exercises and breathing techniques. Ta Mo was allegedly the son of Indian King Sugandha and as such was a member of the warrior caste. Consequently, most authorities agree that he received some sort of martial-arts training throughout his youth. According to legend, when Ta Mo arrived at the Shaolin Temple he found the monks in such poor physical shape that they were incapable of staying awake through the long hours of meditation that he required. Thus he introduced a set of eighteen exercises into their regimen meant to condition and develop their bodies and minds in much the way that hatha yoga does. Known as both "18 Movements of the Arhan Hands" and "18-Monk Boxing," these exercises were basically therapeutic and meditative. Authorities believe that these were the forerunner of Shaolin kung fu from which many of today's forms of the art developed. These exercises proved so popular with his students that other authorities insist that Ta Mo is also responsible for several additional exercise courses. Known as the "Sinew Changing Course" and the "Marrow Washing Course," these exercises (like 18-Monk Boxing) served to strengthen vital internal organs and prevent disease.

Yet, it was only after Ta Mo's death in A.D. 557, that Shaolin kung fu began to come into its own as a fighting art. During the early Tang Dynasty (seventh and eighth centuries A.D) the monks of the Shaolin Monastery were asked to help combat an invasion. They acquitted themselves with such astonishing ease that they instantly became famous for their skill throughout China. Then in the Hou Tang Dynasty (A.D. 705-907) a monk named Sze Hungpey devised the "Feinting Hand" technique that introduced legerdemain to the art. This form of visual trickery further elevated the Shaolin techniques, making them possibly the most formidable in the land.

With the arrival of the Sung Dynasty (960-1127) the importance of the Shaolin Monastery inexplicably began to fade. The founder and emperor of the dynasty, Sung Tai Jo, was himself a master of kung fu. As he is credited with originating the highly respected "Long Fist" style (still practiced today, and long recognized as one of the major branches of the art), it is possible that he contributed to Shaolin's decline.

Late in the Sung dynasty a famous general named Yao Fei (1103-1142) made further improvements in the art based on weapons techniques. Yao Fei, an expert in lance fighting, used this knowledge as a model for his own form of hand-to-hand combat. Later named "Yao's Shan Shou" by his disciples, today it is known as the eagle claw system. Besides its importance as a major school, this is the first *recorded* instance of weapons techniques being used as a model for unarmed combat. Using these unarmed techniques, later pupils originated still another famous branch currently called "Yee Chuen," which translates intriguingly as "Intellectual Fist."

The next major development further accelerated the drift away from the Shaolin style and, according to some sources, almost caused the total extinction of this once-dominant form. Tradition tells us that during the years 1417-1459 a Taoist monk named Chang San-fung devised a radically new form of kung fu known as the "soft fist" or "internal style." Unlike all the forms of kung fu that had gone before, this style was performed slowly and with little apparent physical effort. Up until this point no such division of kung fu existed. All forms of the art were rigorous, sweat-producing exercises that depended upon brute strength to accomplish their purpose. From now on all kung fu was neatly labeled either soft fist or internal style, or hard fist or external style, as the more physical forms came to be known. This was precisely what Chang had in mind, as he felt that all the intense physical exertion which had long been associated with kung fu was contrary to the spirit of Taoism and Buddhism, and in particular conflict with the various health nourishing exercises that had been long associated with the art. Consequently, he developed a style composed of graceful ballet-like movements which from all outward appearances scarcely looked like a martial art. Although Chang's innovative internal school literally shook the kung fu world, it eventually developed into a handful of styles (compared to virtually hundreds of external styles), of which tai chi chuan is the best known. The soft fist techniques were to have an influence totally out of proportion to their numbers, and the initial success of Chang's teachings almost drove the Shaolin school to the verge of extinction!

Yet, the Shaolin school was not a flash in the pan, and one hundred years later made a dramatic comeback that forever altered kung fu. Sometime between A.D. 1522 and 1566, a wealthy young man named Yen took the name Chueh Yuan and became a priest at the Shaolin Temple. An expert swordsman as well as a superb hand-to-hand fighter, he revised the work of all his Shaolin predecessors and compacted them into seventy-two deadly styles. But Chueh Yuan was not to be content until the Shaolin art was completely restored to its former glory. Consequently, he traveled throughout the mainland looking for famous kung fu experts who would share their secrets with him to further refine the art. One day he came upon a sixty-year-old peddler who was being roughed up by a sadistic bully. The old peddler consistently tried to "turn the other cheek" but the brute was out for blood. Before anyone could intervene, the bully lashed out at the old peddler with a savage kick. Yet, the old man merely touched his foot with two fingers of his right hand and the bully fell unconscious.

Impressed, Chueh Yuan immediately revealed his quest. The peddler, whose name was Li Chieng, modestly explained that he did not have any great knowledge of the martial arts, but he offered to introduce him to Pai Yu-feng, the acknowledged master of Shansi, Honan, and Hopeh—provinces that comprised a sizable hunk of China.

At the time, Pai was fifty and at the height of his power. With a reputation as a kindly, spiritual man, Pai received Chueh warmly and listened openly to his plans for the advancement of kung fu. He was impressed by the young man's expertise and burning desire to elevate the art and agreed to accompany Chueh to the Shaolin Temple. There they enlarged and refined Chueh's 72 movements into 170 actions which were subdivided into five animal styles or forms. Each form was made up of a set number of actions that imitated the movements of the dragon, tiger, leopard, snake, and crane. Each form represented the cultivation of one of the five "essences" that Pai believed all men possessed. The dragon style is designed to nurture the spirit. The tiger style trains the bones to resist heavy shock. The leopard style develops strength. The crane style trains the sinews. The snake style is for building *chi*. Pai's program had an enormous impact on the art for two reasons. First, it combined the best aspects of the soft fist with the hard fist. Second, its animal forms became the basis of many of the schools that exist in China today. Yet, despite this striking advancement, the Shaolin art was almost totally destroyed scarcely a century later. This was no simple decline, but the result of an invasion by a powerful border tribe, the Manchus. By 1644 the conquest was complete, the Ming dynasty was ousted and the Ch'ing dynasty installed.

This initiated almost three hundred years of rebellion in which Ming sympathizers and patriots went underground in an attempt to throw off the yoke of "foreign domination." During the early years of these efforts the Shaolin Temple became a virtual hotbed of revolution. It was an ideal vehicle for secrecy and military training. The effectiveness of using a monastery for a refuge was attributed to the special treatment accorded monks and nuns by Chinese society. While an ordinary citizen was subject to the laws of the country, a monk was not. Curiously, this was because monks were no longer considered members of Chinese society. A worshipper of God was not of the material world. Such a person was called *sh'u-shia* and his name was often deleted from family records because it was widely considered a disgrace to leave society. Thus the loyalists were free to enter monastery life, invent new defense systems, and train others in the arts of war.

The true monks, naturally, resented this invasion, and tried unsuccessfully to weed out the loyalists. The same stratagem of infiltration was used at other monasteries which led to the persecution of Buddhists and Taoists by the Manchu emperor, K'ang-hsi, who forbade his subjects to worship in these temples. The entire situation came to a head when an informer told the Manchus of the Shaolin Temple's whereabouts and of the martial trainings that the Mings were administrating. The emperor sent an army to the monastery to arrest all that were involved in the plot. Knowing their fate, the monks fought brilliantly and repulsed the Manchu forces. But K'ang-hsi could not allow a nest of revolution to exist or such a humiliating defeat to go unpunished. A subsequent and larger attack was mounted which totally destroyed the monastery. Bent on revenge, the Manchu forces massacred all but five of the monks. These five escaped, taking with them the secret of the Shaolin art. And within a short space of time, with the aid of other Ming loyalists, they built a second Shaolin monastery whose sole goal was revolution.

Unfortunately, history often repeats itself, and the Manchus learned of the second monastery. Again they dispatched an enormous force against it but with a different outcome. This time most of the monks had been informed of the attack and were able to escape. They fled to the southern cities and began to disseminate their knowledge to make a living and to further their cause. For the first time Shaolin techniques became available to the general public. As a result hundreds of new styles were devised and became the basis of most of the external forms practiced today.

The dispersion produced another fascinating phenomenon particuarly indicative of the dual nature (good and evil) of kung fu—the rise of patriotic secret societies. Formed by loyalists and monks, these societies organized underground governments which channeled their energy into humanitarian as well as political causes. The major group, the Triads, created by the Shaolin monks, even took on the responsibility of educating the young and caring for the elderly. Dr. Sun Yat-sen, the founder of the short-lived Chinese Republic, was an important Triad, and is responsible for founding the Hong Kong branch. From this base, in what was then a British colony, he coordinated the founding of the first and only Chinese democracy.

A darker page of history attributes the infamous "Boxer Rebellions" of 1900 to the secret societies. Essentially an attempt to overthrow the Manchus, the "boxers" were kung fu men who received their training from these societies. Called "boxers," because westerners had no other name for such skill in unarmed combat, the rebellion proved a major setback for kung fu. Thousands were slaughtered, as these valiant kung fu men fought fully equipped western armies sent to prop up the corrupt and crumbling Manchu dynasty.

With the establishment of the republic a few years later, many of these groups lost their patriotic motivation. Different factions of the once-esteemed Triads began to battle each other for the control of towns and tracts of territory. The disintegration continued until more and more groups turned to crime and harassment. The infamous and bloody tong wars of San Francisco were a direct outgrowth of this rivalry.

The low point of Triad activity was reached during World War II. After the Japanese invasion, the military authorities controlling Hong Kong successfully elicited aid from the Triads. Under Japanese protection the Triads united and formed a single gang called the Hung Ah Kee Kwan (Asia Flourishing Association). The Japanese virtually gave the Triads Hong Kong, where they ran all vice operations until the end of the war. Returning authorities managed to destroy the Triads through infiltration in the early 1950s, yet many of the arriving immigrants in the United States and elsewhere still have some secret society background, which explains the resurgence of gang activities in Chinatowns across the country.

The history of the Triads is by no means unique in kung fu annals. Other secret patriotic societies and principled kung fu schools have experienced a similar process of degeneration. The Triads stand out from all the other offshoots of the prestigious Shaolin Temple and make kung fu's dual nature all the more apparent.

Returning to the history and development of the art, the final and most recent innovations were to come from the internal school. Although the original "soft fist" as taught by the legendary monk Chang San-fung was lost, a new and immensely important style developed sometime in the eighteenth century. According to spoken record, a man named Wang Tsung-yueh was passing through a small town in Honan when he saw the villagers practicing their own regional form of kung fu. Later, at an inn, Wang made a number of remarks about this style, and he was immediately challenged by several of the villagers. He dispatched his challenges with such ease that the impressed elders of the village asked him to stay and teach them his "soft fist" techniques. Wang accepted their invitation and their town, Ch'en chia kou, became the center from which modern tai chi developed. In subsequent years tai chi was to develop into three distinct schools. The oldest branch was called the Ch'en school, named after the Ch'en family clan who were almost the sole inhabitants of the Honan village (Ch'en chia kou) where Wang taught his soft fist defense. That Wang actually existed is a certainty; who he learned his art from is a mystery. All we have today to authenticate his teachings is a brief but impressive manual he wrote sometime in the late 1700s. Unfortunately, Wang's original system is lost, but the Ch'en clansmen further developed tai chi into two methods which gradually spread throughout China over the next few centuries.

Tai chi was not the only "soft fist" school that developed: in the same period is hsing-i, also called lu-ho chuan and i-chuan. Roughly translated as mind-fist, or heart-mind fist, all the names purposely suggest that physical action developed to its highest point is at one with the mind. The originator of the school is unknown, but its history begins with Chi Lung-feng who, between 1637 and 1661, met a strange boxer who taught him this unique form. Chi had two major students, one an important general in Shansi and the other a kung fu man in Honan who gradually spread the art throughout China. Perhaps the most significant event in the evolution of hsing-i was its collision with another internal system called pa-kua, with which it eventually coupled. Today, both systems are usually taught together as complementary methods.

Pa-kua is the last major form of internal kung fu to be developed. Devised some time in the early nineteenth century, it is very mystical and difficult to master. Based on the ancient *Book of Changes* or *I Ching*, it stresses (as the book does) the cyclical nature of all things. Consequently, the basic movements are circular, and the chief exercise is called "walking the circle."

Kung fu did not stop developing with pa-kua. Many other new and ingenious styles were invented; however, their overall impact on the direction of the art has been slight. But with the recent resurgence of the art and the new spirit of cooperation, startling new developments further enlarging the abilities of the kung fu man may be around the corner.

3
Kung Fu Customs and Training

Traditional kung fu, with its emphasis on developing the total man, is rare in most occidental countries. Too many kung fu parlors have become little more than self-defense schools with scant emphasis on meditation, philosophy, and health practices. In the West, admission into a kung fu school is relatively simple—put your money down and sign the register. To some extent, the same sort of profiteering even goes on today in Hong Kong and Taiwan. This was by no means the case a few hundred years ago, when the art was at its zenith. In those days, gaining entrance, living in the school, and graduating was a serious business that few survived. There were continual tests to be passed, customs to be observed, and rituals to be performed—all upon the pain of instant dismissal although in a somewhat altered form. Now that admission and day-to-day existence in a kung fu school is no longer the ordeal it once was, many of the time-honored tricks and tests serve another purpose—determining which students can be trusted with advanced knowledge. Thus these descriptions present a reasonably accurate picture of how kung fu men lived, and in some ways still live among other kung fu men.

THE TEST OF ACCEPTANCE

The prospective student, after selecting which style of the art he wishes to learn, visits a master of that school in the hope of being accepted. He is instructed to wait outside the master's quarters (usually housed within a compound that comprises the school) shortly before sunrise. Upon his arrival, the prospect frequently discovers a number of other men also wishing instruction. All are kept waiting a long time, during which their patience and temper undergo the first of many tests. Water or dirt may be "accidentally" thrown on them. Regular students ignore them or treat them rudely. Then after many hours they are told that there will be a delay because of an important ceremony the master must perform. Finally, they are told to go home because the master will not be able to see them that day. Those who display any kind of anger or petulance are immediately dismissed and told never to return.

The next day, for the benefit of those who still seek instruction, the entire procedure is repeated. In addition to the usual humiliations, they are under constant secret surveillance to determine whether they are nervous, talkative, or argumentative among themselves. After many hours they are asked to kneel, and the master appears briefly. He doesn't say a word, but merely looks them over. If any of the prospects rush toward him, or try to talk, they are asked to leave because they have not shown respect to their elders.

As the days drag by, those who remain are insulted, continually asked what they are doing there and finally asked to go home. If they are still not discouraged they are assigned menial tasks like scrubbing the floor. Then, on cue, just prior to the completion of their work, some of the regular students walk across the floor with muddy shoes. Another ploy is to chastise the prospect for not cleaning up areas he was not assigned. After these and other chores are done, all the prospect can expect is still more dirty work—all again with an eye toward devotion and even-tempered behavior.

Eventually, they are asked to eat breakfast with the members of the school. First, each prospective student is given a cracker but is told not to eat it. Some do, but the wiser ones do not. Then they are given a small bottomless bowl, but only the foolish question this strange choice of eating implement. Next they are served rice soup; those who ask how they are to eat the soup are immediately dismissed. All prospects who question are considered unintelligent and unresource-ful, thus not be trusted with the secrets of the school. The wise ones who are patient and do not eat their cracker know to place it at the bottom of the bowl. When the soup is passed, they pour it into the now functional bowl.

Those who pass the breakfast test are assigned to work in the kitchen. Here their control is further tested by how they work with others and how they work while doing difficult tasks. At the end of their kitchen stay they are asked to kill and prepare a white rabbit (the white rabbit is considered a revered animal, and to eat it would be a major gaffe). The correct response is to risk a beating rather than kill the animal.

Next the prospects are tested for honesty. This is accomplished by giving them some money for a specific purpose. Later, it is decided that it is no longer necessary for the prospect to have the money and he is asked to return it. They are then given back part of the money and told that they returned more than the original sum. If the student accepts the additional money he is dismissed. A similar test is also repeated with various beads or mementos, except upon the return of these items the prospect is accused of not returning the original number given. Here he is judged according to how he deals with the situation.

Those who remain are then given an endurance test. The prospect is asked to assume the arduous horse stance in the sun during the hottest part of the day.

Moreover, he must maintain the stance until a lengthy stick of incense burns itself out. Anyone not capable of enduring the pain and discomfort is judged as insincere and not sufficiently motivated.

Finally, the survivors are asked to a formal audience with the master. Here they are requested to drink a cup of tea with the master, thereby becoming full-fledged students. The master himself pours the tea, but if any of them drink it they are immediately told to leave. The rationale for this abrupt dismissal is that by permitting the master to serve them, they have reduced his role to one of a servant, which implies that they know more than the master. The correct etiquette is to approach the altar of the ancestors (every school has one) and pour the tea out in three smooth strokes, saying, "I honor the ancestors and the master that is before me and the masters who I do not know but who have contributed to the knowledge of mankind." Next, the student should have refilled his cup and said, "Having honored the masters before my time, I now honor the present master who I hope I am worthy to serve." If the master is satisfied, he then drinks his tea and the survivors become full-fledged pupils.

LIFE IN A KUNG FU SCHOOL

At this point, the accepted pupils embark on an entirely new existence, so much so that they are advised to forget much of their previous lives. Toward this end, they are often given a new name by which they will be known in this particular "family of men." The school now becomes the student's "family" and there is a rigid structure by which all must abide. A student's teacher (the master only teaches the advanced students) is called the instructor father or father teacher. If married, this man's wife is known as the instructor mother or mother teacher. Students who have preceded new members are known as older brothers—regardless of their actual age. Similarly, students who are later accepted are referred to as little brothers. Other teachers who belong to the same class as the instructor are called uncles, and their students are called teacher nephews.

The daily routine varies greatly among schools. In some the students live at home, in others they live within the school. In some they are required to work the master's grounds, and in others they simply pay a tuition. In monasteries, there are work periods, group meditation, single meditation, study periods, rituals, and services to attend. Thus, with the vast amount of differences among schools, to try to construct a typical day would be a precarious undertaking. Suffice it to say that most serious schools have one thing in common: The day starts early, usually at sunrise, is celebrated in group meditation or chant, then divided among work, study, practice, and meditation, and ends at sunset. Normally the student follows this schedule of activity for close to ten years before he is (if then) considered proficient to teach on his own. Dropouts from this strenuous grind are commonplace and few who are accepted complete their studies. Students leave for other reasons, the most common, to expand their catalog of styles. Consequently students who had studied with a dozen masters are commonplace, although not necessarily the most knowledgeable. The real secrets of the art are usually withheld for years, until the master is absolutely sure that he can trust the man, and even then passed on to only a few select pupils.

GRADUATION

Graduation from the famed Shaolin Temple was even more difficult than from most schools. Here a student had to pass three tests, and he was a virtual prisoner who was not permitted beyond the gate until he passed them. First, there was a difficult oral examination on the art's history, theory, and significant Chinese thought. Next, he had to acquit himself favorably in actual competition with several colleagues. Finally, there was a harrowing ordeal involving a booby-trapped hallway and 108 mechanized wooden dummies. As the student worked his way through the hall, the dummies, each equipped with knives, spears, and clubs, would attack him in a random fashion. This was accomplished by ingenious mechanical devices beneath the corridor floor that were triggered by the student's own weight. The monks who devised these devilish devices arranged them in such a manner that they were totally unpredictable. Consequently, it was possible to trigger two, four, or more dummies at the same time. If the student succeeded in working his way through this hall, he was faced with one more obstacle—a smoldering five-hundred-pound urn that blocked his exit. Naturally, there was a prescribed manner for moving the urn. The student was expected to hug it with his forearms in such a way that the two sculpted symbols of its side, the dragon and the tiger, would be burned into his flesh. Once he completed this test he was at last free to leave, and his branded forearms brought him great respect and honor wherever he traveled.

Many students failed these rigid tests and were not permitted to graduate. Hu Wei-ch'uan was such a man. He had entered the Shaolin Temple after being severely beaten by his enemies, and stayed fifteen years trying to master the art. Finally he passed the first two tests, but his attempts to get through the booby-trapped corridor never took him farther than the thirty-second dummy. On the last occasion, he was carried out, doctored, and returned to his quarters. Determined to return to his family, he managed to sneak out of the monastery through a sewer duct. Despite his inability to pass the final test, he was more than capable of avenging himself against those who had wronged him. But even more important, according to legend, his escape helped perpetuate the Shaolin techniques which were, in part, lost after the Manchus destroyed the monastery. His technique, called Hua-ch'uan, meaning flowery hands, is a stunning method to watch, composed of many complex and graceful hand movements.

There are a number of other miscellaneous customs that are essential for those embarking on the kung fu

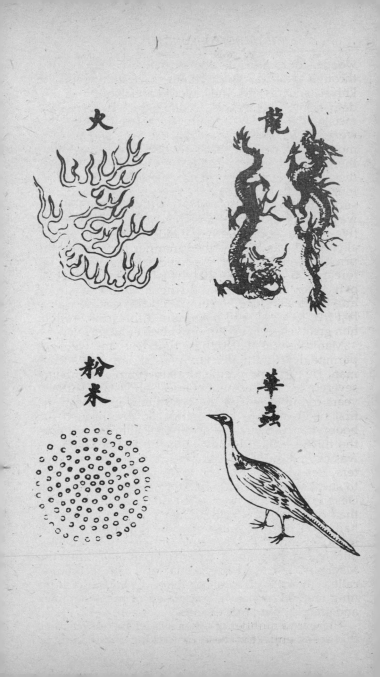

火

龍

粉末

華蟲

journey. First, the kung fu uniform must be worn correctly. This is very similar to the judo uniform, except that it is black. A long sash is worn around the waist, and while most are black some are very colorful. Usually tied into a knot, the sash is worn on the left side by males and the right side by females. A master, on the other hand, wears the knot in the middle. Anyone else who ties his sash in the middle and is not a master is inviting a challenge and possibly a serious beating.

Second, etiquette is essential while visiting another master's hall. If you are offered tea by the master, and you drink it, he is justified in asking you for a bout. To drink his tea, just like drinking your own master's tea before acceptance, is an insult, except, in this case, he will think that you came to his hall solely to challenge him.

Third, the kung fu salute is another important bit of etiquette by which kung fu men recognize and honor each other. Not to salute in most situations is also a grave insult. It is performed by bringing the right fist up into the left palm at roughly chin level while simultaneously bowing the head and upper torso. In a master's hall, and before and after practice sessions, the picture or shrine of the previous master is saluted in this manner.

While there are many other customs that kung fu men follow they are mostly regional in nature. These are the essentials which bind all schools of the art together.

4

Popular Kung Fu Techniques

Five thousand years of evolution have produced an enormous variety of schools and styles. Yet from this confusion of techniques the casual observer is able to discern that kung fu is polarized along two distinctly different lines—the hard and soft fist styles. Traditionally, the hard fist style relied on technique and brute strength, and the soft fist on graceful motions and inner strength. However, in recent years these simple demarcation lines have blurred. While many hard fist styles still rely on raw strength, most of them have embraced the soft fist method of calling up internal energy. Consequently, modern-day hard fist styles place considerable emphasis on breathing and meditational techniques. Of course, this cross fertilization in the art works both ways. The soft fist school has picked up a number of the hard school linear striking methods and footwork, in addition to the use of weapons for training and body development. Despite the convergent evolution there are a goodly number of differences in the two approaches that are worthy of note.

民相敵鬭圖

First, the external school is based heavily on technique and has many more styles than the internal school. There are presently 360 documented styles of external kung fu. How many more exist is anyone's guess, as individual family clans have held their styles secret for centuries. This markedly contrasts with the four styles of internal kung fu, of which tai chi is the most widely practiced.

Second, the hard school is characterized by rhythm, leaps, speed, and spectacular hand and foot actions. The soft school, on the other hand, is exemplified by slow motion movements that imperceptibly blend from one into another. Moreover, the hands and feet are never involved in any acrobatic displays, but in tai chi are lightly kept in contact with one's opponent throughout the bout. Thus while the hard school utilizes brisk, calisthenic-like movements, the soft school teaches a more elegant, ballet-like motion.

Third, among Chinese, the people who perform the hard and soft styles usually are split along rigid age lines. Since the soft fist does not demand the considerable expenditure of physical energy that the hard fist requires, those who practice it are generally older. The hard school, on the other hand, is widely preferred by the young because it is easier to learn, and more spectacular to perform. The comparative ease with which the hard fist is learned has resulted in its adoption by the Chinese army as a means of physical training and personal combat. However, it is widely recognized that most Chinese as they grow older turn their attention to the internal methods.

Fourth, while it is true that the system is only as good as the man, it is generally acknowledged that the soft fist is the more efficacious form of fighting. This only stands to reason because perfection in any style of the internal school often takes about twenty years, while a style of the external school can usually be mastered in less than half that time.

Fifth, internal kung fu is allegedly more healthy than the external forms. While there is virtually no way of proving this statement, it is known that the internal exercises combined with breathing techniques are an excellent means of preventive medicine and are startlingly beneficial for treating a wide variety of ailments from high blood pressure to stomach and lung ailments. Of course many of the hard-school masters make similar, although unvalidated, claims for their techniques. And since they now utilize many of the same techniques as the internal school there is no doubt some truth in them. Yet, twenty years of testing in a number of hospitals and sanitariums on mainland China have definitely proved the efficacy of the internal approach.

Sixth, internal school tactics were devised solely as a means of self-defense, while the external school methods are for offense as well as defense. In the internal schools, the practitioner uses his opponent's force to create counter force. If the opponent does not attack, he will not be harmed because he has generated no force. But if he does attack, through circular motions all his energy is turned against himself! Thus a man who attacks with enough power to break someone's arm will in turn have his own arm broken! Or if he attacks with the intent to kill, he may end up as the dying victim. For the most part, the external school possesses no such techniques, and their methods can be classified as either defensive (blocking) or offensive (attacking).

Despite the many differences between schools they are all still kung fu. And from these diverse schools a number of distinctive styles have come to currently dominate kung fu. As such, they are of immense interest for their legends and anecdotes, as well as for their combative techniques. The rest of this chapter is devoted to a number of thumbnail sketches of some of the popular styles that are now practiced and their evolution and impact on China. First, we shall deal with the external school.

THE EXTERNAL SCHOOL

Most of the external forms that are practiced today can trace their origins back to the famous Shaolin

Temple. Although destroyed by the Manchus in the seventeenth century, the escaped Shaolin monks systematized the art into five basic styles. These five, in turn, have gone through untold changes producing countless methods. Hung gar kung fu, unlike most of the subsequent styles that developed, claims to be the original, unadulterated form taught at the Temple. The reason for the art's alleged purity harks back to its founder, Hung Geee Gung, who spent most of his life studying under two Shaolin monks. One of his teachers, Chee Sin, was a master of the long hand methods taught at the monastery; the other, Fong Wing Chuen, was skillful in the short hand art. Hung combined their teachings to faithfully reconstruct the methods taught at Shaolin. Today the school is based on the five animal actions devised by Pai Yu-feng and Chueh Yuan (who revitalized the art in the fourteenth century) with particular emphasis on the tiger and crane styles. Students of this school learn a lengthy series of movements which look like some form of a Chinese classical dance. In actuality these forms, called kata by the Chinese, imitate the defensive and offensive moves made by the animals while under attack. For example, although the leopard and tiger appear to be from the same family, their methods of attacks are quite different. This is mirrored in each specific kata. In the leopard kata, the leopard's paw delivers a fore-knuckle strike, while the tiger's claw (in the tiger kata) is a fierce open-palmed hit, coupled with a raking motion. According to experts in this style, each dance or kata requires three years of practice before it can be successfully applied as a method of self-defense. But before the beginner is even permitted to learn the various kata he goes through a rigorous training period to get his body in shape. The student's first goal is to develop a solid stance from which to practice the katas. For six months he is expected to practice the arduous horse stance, holding this difficult position for as long as forty-five minutes a day. An ancient proverb best sums up the necessity of the horse stance by saying: "Before you can learn to defeat others, you must first learn to stand."

At the end of this period not only are the student's legs stronger, but his center of gravity is lowered, turning him into an immovable obstacle for the average man. In addition to this training, the student is also expected to be developing his inner powers, called hee gun in this school. Being physically strong is not nearly enough; raising *chi* is considered vastly superior, as well as being highly valued for its health-giving aspects. Thus anyone interested in learning traditional Shaolin kung fu is in for an enormous amount of work, combined with an extensive program of physical exercise.

THE PRAYING MANTIS SCHOOL. Like many forms of kung fu this school owes its development to the study of how other forms of life defend themselves—in this case insects. According to legend, Wang Lang, an expert swordsman, lived sometime during the Ming dynasty (1368-1644). At that time, it was common knowledge that the Shaolin monks were unexcelled in the field of martial art. Wang considered himself invincible and was anxious to prove this to all so he decided to challenge the monasteries' best. To his great surprise he was soundly beaten by a monk of the lowest rank. Determined to better himself, he went into seclusion and practiced continuously. When he returned to Shaolin, he won repeatedly until he fought the more experienced monks, who thoroughly beat him. Discouraged and disgusted with himself, he wandered off into the open country to soothe his wounded ego. Suddenly, his thoughts were interrupted by a shrill, piercing noise emanating from a tree above his head. Intrigued, Wang climbed the tree until he came upon a curious sight. A praying mantis was battling a large cicada. At first, the mantis looked very fragile and helpless compared to its large foe, but on closer examination it became apparent that the cicada was actually on the receiving end, as the shrewd movements of the mantis' sickle-like front feet overwhelmed it. Wang was fascinated by the mantis' form of attack and promptly captured the insect to further observe it. By feeding it live insects and by provoking it with a piece of straw, Wang soon learned the secrets of the animal's defense. Inspired by what he discovered, Wang gradually devised a unique method of attack and defense based on the tactics of the mantis. His new method was divided into three categories that he was certain would defeat even the most experienced of adversaries. The first, called p'eng p'u, was devised to keep an opponent off balance. The second, lan t'seh, checked an opponent's attack and broke down his strength. The third, p'a tsou, was the murderous eight elbow attack, designed to end the match.

Armed with his new bag of tricks, Wang trained intensively before returning to Shaolin. This time he was unstoppable as monk after monk fell before his new techniques. He became an instant hero at the monastery, and all the monks begged him to teach them his new style. Buoyed by his success, he set up his own school and, as the word of his phenomenal victory spread throughout the country, hundreds of disciples flocked to his door. His dream fulfilled years later, Wang died an old, rich, and famous warrior.

Over the centuries the praying mantis form continued to develop, but like many other schools it was plagued by factionalism. Eventually, it split into four schools, of which the tai t'si emerged as the foremost. The founder of this particular branch, Liang Tsu, was so highly regarded by other martial artists that, on his eightieth birthday, seven of the leading martial artists presented him with a complete codification of their best tactics. Two of these methods, one on breath strategy and the other on ground-level attack, were incorporated into Liang Tsu's system and are still with us today.

For the uninitiated, watching an expert practice this method is amusing. The katas, which are between forty and one hundred movements long, actually do imitate the mantis. The hands are frequently positioned in a way that resembles the two front feelers of the insect, and the fast elusive footwork also simulates the way the mantis hops about. But there is nothing funny about the devastation those funny movements can unleash on an unwary opponent.

Today, the numerous styles are still very popular on mainland China, Taiwan, and with Chinese throughout the world.

DRUNKEN STYLE. As the name suggests, this particular branch of kung fu is patterned on the movements of someone who has had a few too many. The practitioner stumbles around his opponent in a seemingly random pattern and in some cases even falls and rolls around on the ground. Yet, all this is a clever ruse, designed to make the practitioner a difficult target—one whose whereabouts is always uncertain. Just when the opponent is most confused, the practitioner comes in low and lashes out with a sudden flurry of kicks and blows. Attacks are often launched while lying on the ground; consequently, the style relies heavily on foot techniques.

This type of defense is similar to an even more esoteric style, known as lost track. Here the practitioner confounds his enemy by disappearing before his eyes. There is nothing supernatural about this technique; the practitioner merely utilizes a series of feints whereby he ends up behind his opponent.

As for the origin of the drunken style, no one is sure how, where, or why it came into being. Naturally, there are a number of popular myths, which, although worth repeating, should not be taken as authenticated fact. One story credits Li Po, one of China's most famous bards, as the father of the system. This is by no means inconceivable as Li Po was a pretty wild character. Fond of swordplay and martial arts in general, he was a notorious wine drinker. Much of his verse commemorates his romance with the grape which no doubt contributed to the popular belief that he devised the drunken style.

Another tale claims that the system was discovered in an old manuscript in the famous Eight

Fairies. This seems to be corroborated by the fact that one branch of this school is called the "eight fairies style." Regardless of from whom or where it came, it is predominantly practiced inside Communist China, and it is all but unknown outside the mainland.

For skeptics who think that this system offers little in the way of control, experts like to demonstrate their art. While holding a glass of water, they will wildly stagger around an opponent, fall, roll on the ground, do a somersault, knock the legs out from under their target, and leap to their feet—all while never spilling a drop from their glass!

CHOY LI FUT. Developed only 140 years ago for warfare, this style was an outgrowth of the ever-present Chinese desire to rid themselves of the hated Manchus. The patriots of the era needed a technique that could turn out experts in the shortest possible time—choy li fut was their answer. Ironically, it is roughly analogous to the type of hand-to-hand combat taught in our own military services. It is a style composed of roundhouse swings, hooks, uppercuts, and kicks—all utilized in a highly original manner. There are even a number of startling similarities between it and western-style boxing.

Since their Manchu foes were well armed, students also trained extensively with the wide variety of medieval weaponry that was then prevalent. As armed techniques were an extension of basic hand techniques, weapons training played a dual role strengthening the student in each area.

Choy li fut is yet another offshoot of the famous Shaolin style. Chan Heung, the founder of the school, studied under two Shaolin monks, Choy and Li. When Chan formulated his new system he decided to honor his teachers by naming it in their honor, hence choy and li. The fut at the end was added because it means Buddha, thereby paying homage to the monastery from which much of his art sprang.

While there are virtually hundreds of other hard fist methods in wide use—the eagle claw system, cha k'un, law horn k'un, wah k'un, and monkey style, just to name a few—to cover them fully would prove an exhaustive examination. Yet, the aforementioned examples should demonstrate the enormous variety to be found in the external art regarding origin, history, techniques, and purpose. The internal school, on the other hand, does not even begin to possess this variety—not because it is by any means inferior, but simply because it is difficult to master and has not been around anywhere as long as the external school. The following four systems comprise the entire internal school, as well as their significant branches.

THE INTERNAL SCHOOL

TAI CHI CHUAN. This style is currently the most popular form of the enigmatic soft fist techniques. To most westerners tai chi is not a form of martial arts, but a series of dance-like health exercises. While it is true that tai chi is beneficial to the health, it is first and foremost a means of self-defense, each posture having a definite fighting function. Considered by many as the best means to ward off an attacker, martial arts tournaments are frequently won by tai chi masters. Even the name of the system, tai chi chuan, indicates its martial bent since it translates as grand ultimate fist.

The serious student is expected to learn the art on three levels. Kung-chia, or solo exercise, is but the first step. When the student becomes more advanced he practices t'iu-shou, or pushing hands, a two-man exercise which trains the student never to lose contact with his opponent's hands, enabling him to anticipate a move before it happens. San-shou, or free fighting, is the third level, and it is exactly what the name implies, a sparring match in which the student learns to react to the unexpected. A fourth level would be a self-defense application of the above three if a threatening situation should actually arise.

Since its inception, tai chi has undergone many changes and modifications. In some methods there are as many as 108 or 128 movements in a kata. In other methods the number of movements has been reduced to 37. In 1956, the Peking All China Physical Training Society further reduced the number to 24 movements which the government then utlized in its national physical fitness program. Depending on what style you use, it takes anywhere from five to twenty-five minutes to go through an entire kata.

Currently, there are three major schools of tai chi, with a number of minor offshoots. First, there is the original ch'en school refined by the Ch'en clan who inhabited the small town in Honan where Wang Tsung-yueh first taught. There are reputedly two ch'en styles, one old and one new, of which the new is almost extinct. The second branch was founded by Yang Lu-ch'an who was the first outsider allowed to learn the ch'en art. He learned the old style and improved on it twice before teaching it to his sons who passed it on to the rest of the world. Known as the yang style, it is reputedly the most practiced form in China today, and the form that the government saw fit to modify to twenty-four movements for its citizens. Both these systems were learned by Wu Yu-hsiang sometime in the nineteenth century. Late in life he created his own style, from the new ch'en and old yang, known as the wu style. This form is more difficult than the preceding forms, and consequently there are few who practice it. This wu style should not be confused with a later branch of the yang style also called wu, which enjoys considerable popularity.

The principles by which one masters tai chi are unique, particularly for a martial art. First, and above all, the student must be totally relaxed. Utilizing breathing techniques, the strength and weight of the body are "emptied" from the chest and permitted to sink to the soles of the feet until the student feels rooted to the ground. Second, the waist must be flexible and supplely enters and is part of every movement. Third, the body must be held so lightly that a fly lighting on it would not only be felt but would set the body in motion. Fourth, every movement is circular. Circular movements build *chi* and are the best means of neutralizing an incoming force.

The health benefits of tai chi are legendary. Masters of the art claim salutory effects on the nervous system (through meditation), the cardio-vascular and digestive systems (through diaphragm breathing), the reproductive systems (through specific movements that tonify the genitals), and the musculoskeletal system. Tai chi is also of enormous benefit to those suffering posture problems. As such it is widely recommended as an ideal exercise during pregnancy or for those with back disorders.

No discussion of tai chi would be complete without knowledge of the many myths and legends that surround this fascinating art. As you may recall, the legendary founder was a Taoist monk named Chang Sen-Fung, and like many before him, he too was originally inspired by the actions of animals. The story goes that Chang, a fourteenth-century Taoist philosopher, witnessed a curious battle. A bird of prey, noticing a snake beneath him, dove on its intended victim. The snake, seeing the bird, dodged the bird's efforts by skillfully circling its head. The bird dove again and again, but each time the snake easily circled past. The snake then feigned weakness, and the curious bird came closer. No sooner was the bird in range then the snake struck, burying its fangs deep into the surprised bird. Fascinated by the snake's easy avoidance of the bird, Chang memorized its circular movements, then painstakingly worked out a system of defense that reputedly became the forerunner of tai chi.

According to experts, there are three types of tai chi strength—on a plane, on a straight line, and on a point. The third, and the most effective, was possessed by Yang Lu-ch'an, the founder of the famous yang branch. Reputedly he passed it on to his sons and grandsons, but unfortunately it appears lost to the present generation. Some of the exploits of this type of mystical strength are amazingly colorful. Yang Pan'hou, one of the old master's sons, was challenged to show his famous sticking energy by a southern kung fu master. The challenger placed bricks all around the yard and told Yang to place his right hand, unclenched, on his back. The challenger was to hop from brick to brick, and if Yang's hand came off, he lost. With amazing speed, the man leaped around the scattered bricks in an unpredictable pattern; yet despite his strength and cunning he could not get away from Yang. Finally, in one swift motion he leaped to the roof of a nearby shed and turned to find Yang gone; then as he turned around again, Yang was still with him. And on another occasion when a swallow alighted on Yang's hand it could not fly away because Yang "hearing" its energy would move his palm in such a way that the bird would not have a firm enough base from which to launch itself. Of course, the master of the school himself, old man Yang, was immensely powerful. Legend tells us he once knocked a challenger across the room by merely expelling his breath when the man hit his stomach. Another of his sons was so skillful that he once defeated a famous swordsman with nothing more than a wooden brush.

PA-KUA. No one knows the exact origin of this internal art, but Tung Hai-chuan is the acknowledged father of the system. The story goes that when Tung was a young man he was lost in the mountains of Kiangsu Province. He was nearly dead of starvation and exhaustion when an anonymous Taoist hermit happened upon him and saved his life. As the hermit nourished him back to health he taught Tung a "divine" form of boxing. Tung was so impressed he stayed with the hermit several years until he had mastered pa-kua. He later returned to Peking where he gained considerable fame for his technique. His fame brought a challenge from Kuo Yun-shen of the hsing-i school and resulted in a famous three-day battle. On the first two days neither could achieve an advantage, but on the third day Tung so completely defeated Kuo that they became lifelong friends. They then signed a pact that required hsing-i students to take pa-kua training and vice versa. Consequently, to this day the systems are learned together and are specifically designed to complement each other. Where hsing-i utilized vertical strength, linear movement, and the fist, pa-kua emphasizes horizontal strength, circular movement, and the open palm.

The principal pa-kua exercise consists of walking a circle for about thirty minutes while performing a wide variety of body movements. Paradoxically, there are only eight postures that a student must learn; yet within them there are all the possible movements that the human body can make. By performing these difficult gyrations the student can adjust his body to any necessary situation. This is because pa-kua does not teach fighting tricks or techniques; it simply teaches the practitioner how to move. While other systems have the student imagine his opponent in front of him, pa-kua does not. While other methods emphasize strikes and kicks, pa-kua does not. Instead, defense technique depends solely on the situation; yet, pa-kua is a powerful weapon, constantly baffling opponents with a series of confusing circular steps which enable the student to show up anywhere. And since one of its main goals is to build up internal power, a blow from a pa-kua expert would be devastating.

Pa-kua like tai chi is composed almost solely of circular movements. The rationale behind this is fascinating and instructive. While many other schools believe that the shortest distance between two points is a straight line, both tai chi and pa-kua generally dispute this. They point out since there is no beginning or end to a circle, it is possible to maintain continuous motion. They assert that this is superior to a punch or kick where the student must stop and reverse directions. Moreover, a person who is practicing the linear forms of kung fu has to overcome a greater amount of inertia than a student of the circular forms who initiates his movement from an already flowing pattern. Finally, and most important, the circular moves enable the student to store *chi*, building up a greater and greater amount with every passing year of practice.

The principal goals of pa-kua have less to do with self-defense than any other of the soft fist techniques. The basic interests of most students is the discovery of natural laws through total control of the body by the mind. A controlled and calm mind is the first step, which in turn enables the student to use his will, rather than physical strength to move his body. Thus, in pa-kua training, what a student intellectually understands about movement is transformed into controlled physical instinctual functioning.

Pa-kua is deeply tied up with Taoism, and its movements are based on the mystical *I Ching* or *Book of Changes*. The book is a collection of complex linear signs that were used in divination. The Chinese word for these signs is kua, while pa translates as the number eight, hence the origin of pa-kua which means eight diagrams. The number eight is particularly significant because eight diagrams form the basis of the *I Ching*. Each of these diagrams has a name and an attribute. Pa-kua's founder modeled the eight basic actions of the art on these *I Ching* diagrams. And the movements of pa-kua directly correspond to the attributes of each diagram.

In the area of health, pa-kua masters insist that they can cure a wide variety of disorders: high blood pressure, ulcers, tuberculosis, and arteriosclerosis to name just a few. In general, pa-kua and tai chi make the same claims. And research carried out in China has verified many cases. Unfortunately, not much in the way of additional research has been carried out to explore the scientific basis that underlies these startling cures.

The stories about the incredible powers of the pa-kua masters are legion. Tung, who is credited with founding the school, was once reputed to have been leaning against a wall as he sat in a chair. Suddenly, the wall collapsed, and his frightened students ran to him, fearful that he had been buried. Yet, when the dust cleared, they discovered him sitting in the same chair against a different wall!

Perhaps the most fascinating story about Tung revolves around his funeral. After the service, when his disciples attempted to raise the casket prior to burial, the casket could not be moved. It was if it were rooted to the ground. The students tried again and again, but to no avail. Then, unexpectedly a voice came from inside the casket saying: "As I told you many times, none of you has one-tenth my skill!" Tung, then eighty-four, died and the casket was moved easily.

Another story involving a twentieth-century master, Chang Chao-tung, is more fairly indicative of the powers a pa-kua master can develop. Chang, when sixty, returned to his home to visit his parents. He was soon approached by the leading boxer of the area, a man named Ma, who politely told him that he could withstand his punch. (This is the traditional method of deciding who is the strongest boxer. The idea is that each man gets a free swing at the other's body, and the amount of internal energy behind the blow would indicate who would prevail in an actual fight. The loser of this bout always has the option of asking for a real contest if unsatisfied with the outcome.) Chang said he would oblige but first ordered four students to hold a blanket in back of Ma. He then advised Ma to protect his body with his hands, although he was only going to strike his arm. Then Chang hit Ma's arm with such force that he was not only immediately knocked backward in the blanket, but he pulled four students on top of him! From that day on Ma was a student of Chang's.

HSING-I. Usually taught with pa-kua, this art has a definite martial slant. This is evident in the five main actions of the art which are called splitting, crushing, drilling, pounding, and crossing. In addition there are twelve other actions drawn from the characteristics of animals, some mythical, including: dragon, tiger, monkey, horse, iguana, cock, hawk, snake, eagle, bear, swallow, and ostrich. Unlike other forms of the soft fist, all actions are performed with lightning-like speed.

There are two predominant branches of the art, one originating from Shansi and the other from Honan. Hsing-i is so highly revered that at one point armed convoys passing through the area of Honan, where many hsing-i students resided, did not show their flags or make boisterous noises meant to frighten off would-be attackers in fear of insulting the district.

NOI CUN. More commonly known as the divine technique, this is a very rare form of kung fu practiced by only a handful of adepts. It is not widely taught or particularly popular because it takes the better part of a lifetime to master. And, quite frankly, it strains the credulity of those who are asked to believe that it exists. Simply put, it is a means of generating internal power so enormous one can fell an opponent without actually touching him. As fantastic as this sounds, most kung fu masters insist that such an art exists, and many claim to have witnessed it. One modern master writing in *Karate Illustrated* stated:

" Here in San Francisco lives a one-hundred-seven-year-old-master who is still able to use *noi cun* (the use of internal power) despite his age and the frailty of his body. I personally have seen him demonstrate. In one of his demonstrations, he asked a young man to step to the center of the room. Then, placing himself a few yards away, he stretched forth his arm, palm pointed outward, and concentrated deeply, drawing from within that great force of his *chi*, and within a few moments the lad was staggering backward, pushed off balance by the unseen force radiating from that oustretched hand."

The same master went on to describe other noi cun masters, including one man in Hong Kong who broke a glass vase from across the room.

Unfortunately, it is a dying art, and the few masters that still exist are by and large sequestered on mainland China. As for other talented masters reviving the art, it requires years of deep meditation, as well as considerable solitude and free time to devote to its practice. Most modern masters are forced to spend their time teaching others or earning a living in an increasingly technological society. Consequently they are not able to develop their *chi* to the point where they are capable of performing noi cun. Thus it is left to hermits, monks, and other spiritual people, most of whom have little contact with conventional society.

So ends this brief look into the popular forms that are practiced today. For those who tend to make judgments as to which school or technique is superior, one kung fu master recently said: "There are no secret styles. No better forms. It is simply the amount of training that one puts into whatever style he is learning. Each style has its strong points; none is better than another . . . ."

ESOTERIC KUNG FU PRACTICES

The hot China sun rose with unmistakable fury over the small mountain town of Wang Fu. Inside the town's meeting hall a raucous celebration was in progress. Led by the evil warlord Tang Lu-sing, the all-night revelers were Tang's own men who had just annexed the once-free village. Tang and his gang, drunk with power and wine, were in the process of humiliating the villagers, hoping to goad them into a response that would call for violence. Toward this end, Tang had decreed that the elder of each family must bring his best wine and meats to the banquet, as well as his youngest daughter. The villagers were sick at heart, it had been an evening of selected rape, and the day promised more of the same. Into this den of thugs, one last frail old man approached Tang's table with his offering. Staggering under his heavy load he stumbles and falls across the table, both he and his produce landing on the dreaded warlord's lap. Fear in his eyes, the old man clutches Tang's arm and begs for forgiveness. Tang sweeps him out of the way and has him thrown out the door. The old man lies there for a moment until the thugs have returned to the hall, then picks himself up and strides purposefully away, no longer the timid feeble creature of a few seconds before.

The next day Tang wakes up in agony. His vision is fuzzy, and his gut feels on fire. He pushes himself to his feet, staggers around the room, and falls to his knees coughing blood. He calls for his doctors, but they are perplexed. For the next three days he screams day and night, then dies in his own stink. His men are confused and demoralized; they cannot understand what has happened. Stupid and superstitious, they decide that Tang died of witchcraft. One by one, they slip out of the cursed village.

TIEH-HSUEH. The above dramatization is an example of tieh-hsueh, one of the least known kung fu arts. No great strength is required, as a master of the art can cause illness, damage internal organs, or kill instantaneously simply by touching one or more secret vital points. Moreover, the effect may be delayed from a few hours to a few weeks. Incredible? Not really, because tieh-hsueh is merely an extension of acupuncture. It stands to reason that a powerful medicine (or medical technique) can just as easily kill or cripple. Tieh-hsueh is a highly complicated system, made up of over 240 pressure points whose effectiveness is determined by which of those points are grabbed or struck. In addition, the time of day determines which points may be utilized for maximum result.

Since this is an extraordinarily deadly form, a master only taught this technique to his most peaceful and dedicated students. Besides learning the pressure points, the student was expected to excel in preparing and administering herbs for specific diseases and general health problems. Today, most kung fu students are taught a fraction of this ancient knowledge in what most teachers call striking points. These points are usually the obvious vulnerable areas of the body such as the groin, instep, Adam's apple, etc. Each is hit differently, depending upon the sought-after result. Some are stamped, others knelt against, and still others are hit with a particular part of the anatomy. Many students confuse this very basic knowledge with real tieh-hsueh, but a master of this art rarely needs force, and only uses his deadly touch in the direst of circumstances. Unfortunately, there are few left who possess the real knowledge, and they will most likely take their wealth of information with them to the grave.

AN CH'I. Translated as hidden weapons, these days it is a very rare type of training. Allegedly, some an ch'i schools train their students solely in this technique, to the exclusion of hand-to-hand combat. Here the student is taught to achieve amazing throwing perfection with whatever is at hand—chopsticks, coins, pebbles. In addition, there is also a dependence on all sorts of gadgets including spring-activated sleeve arrows, sharpened coins, throwing arrows, flying stars (weights and ropes), flying claws (sharp metal claws attached to a rope), and many, many more. Because of an ch'i's devious nature either an unarmed attacker of a heavily armed assailant will find himself in serious trouble if he tangles with this type of kung fu man.

Naturally most kung fu men have negative feelings about these gadgets, visualizing years of conventional training going down the drain. Consequently, many reluctant kung fu men felt forced to master an ch'i. As these hidden devices became more commonplace, they were soon used in serious combat as a means of distracting or weakening an opponent. This in turn led to special new training with which the kung fu man sought to develop a second sense to anticipate these deadly creations.

Special techniques which border on the supernormal make up the remainder of the esoteric kung fu practices. None of the following are fighting techniques, but rather methods of strategy or general defense. All of them take years of diligent practice and most have been verified by qualified observers down through the years.

CH'IN KUNG. Translating roughly as light technique, ch'in kung is a number of methods used in overcoming seemingly impossible obstacles. One particular branch is called "lizard technique" which enables a student to scale a wall with nothing more than his hands and feet. Training starts with a pole inclined against a wall for assistance. Gradually, the angle of the pole against the wall is reduced until the student can scale the wall without the pole. In another version of this technique, the student stands with his back against the wall and using only his heels and hands mounts the wall.

Another strange but similar ch'in kung technique is known as "light walk." Here the student practices walking on the rim of a large jar filled with water. Over a long period of time the jar is gradually drained, while the student attempts to walk so lightly that the jar doesn't tip over, even when empty. In another method, the student places sand in a practice area and covers it with thin paper. He then walks on it trying not to disturb the sand underneath. Masters of this technique, such as Yang Lu-ch'an and other tai chi adepts, were reportedly able to walk on snow or grass without leaving any trace.

Ch'in kung training starts young, usually about twelve. In the more rigorous methods the student wears weights such as the "iron-sand vest" and the "iron-sole shoes" while practicing. Consequently, many fantastic feats of jumping and climbing have been reported.

Other miscellaneous methods of training are known as the "iron ox" and the "wooden man." These consist of striking the vulnerable parts of the body in conjunction with breath control to make the body impervious to attack. Similar training is carried on in many kung fu schools where the teachers beat the students so they develop their internal power to the point where they do not feel the assaults. According to experts, this usually takes about six months.

In addition to these verified methods, there are a number of other tricks that many in China believe possible, although there is no verification to support these beliefs. They include:

THE DRAGON CLAW. A method that enables the student to catch birds, as well as penetrate an aggressor's skin with his fingers. This is accomplished by tossing an empty jar into the air and catching it by its throat.

Gradually the jar is filled with sand, and the fingers become filled with power.

CONTRACTING TESTES. Utilizing deep diaphragm breathing techniques, the student is eventually able to draw his testes up, almost into his body so that they cannot be struck during a fight.

WELL FIST. The student assumes the horse posture at midnight and points his fist to a nearby well. In two or three years the student will be able to make the water mildly turbulent. In ten years he will be able to kill an aggressor from afar.

Many other fantastic and not so fantastic claims have been made. The curious thing for the skeptic to remember is that some of them have proved out.

5
Kung Fu Health Practices and Chinese Medicine

Historically speaking, physical well being and kung fu have long been one and the same. Health nourishing was one of the first areas that kung fu encompassed. Consequently the actual development of both arts became closely linked and at times meshed completely. Present-day physical therapy methods, widely utilized in Chinese medicine, have been taken directly from kung fu. Likewise, traditional Chinese medicine is widely studied by kung fu men, both as a means to repair injuries and for body strengthening.

It stands to reason that both arts belong together, as a man who is sound in body will always be able to think, perform, and defend himself better than one who is not in good physical shape. Before we embark further on this discussion a word of caution is in order. Traditional Chinese medicine as practiced by kung fu men and Chinese doctors alike bears no resemblance to western medical science. The classical methods of treatment are medical gymnastics, breathing exercises, herbal remedies, remedial massage, moxibustion, and acupuncture. While not all kung fu men mastered all these diverse skills, they usually were

三兆習吉圖

周公

reasonably proficient in two or more areas. The kung fu master, on the other hand, is usually accomplished in all the above areas and is frequently a doctor of Chinese medicine. The remainder of the chapter will be devoted to an evaluation of each of these techniques as they are all an important part of the kung fu man's arsenal against ill health.

Medical gymnastics are exactly what many kung fu exercises are. Their purpose is primarily preventive —they are meant to keep the entire body in shape. What the Chinese mean by keeping in shape is not exactly what the West means by the same phrase. In western countries, this refers almost exclusively to sleek bodies and bulging muscles. This is quite the opposite from the traditional concerns of Chinese medicine and kung fu. To the oriental mind, keeping in shape means strengthening internal organs, tonifying the nerve and glandular systems, enlarging the capacity of the cardiovascular system, as well as strengthening the skeletal muscles. Consequently, the Chinese have developed a number of systems of medical gymnastics that specifically are designed to accomplish their type of shaping up. They discovered that specific movements, combined with deep breathing exercises slightly enlarged particular internal organs. Further research concluded that bigger organs were stronger. Western science only recently began to show some interest in this theory when Dr. Cooper and the other aerobic experts proved that jogging (a limited form of exercise) was capable of enlarging the cardiovascular system with very favorable results in cases involving heart ailments. This information is by no means news to the Chinese who developed "life prolonging exercises" thousands of years ago. For kung fu men and Chinese doctors, these exercises are the first line of defense against disease and other illness. They reason that a body that is strong inside, as well as outside, is not likely to succumb to illness or wear down quickly.

Breathing techniques go hand in hand with these exercises and are the key to their success. How they function often mystifies most Occidental people; thus a brief explanation will be helpful. If you ask a westerner to take a deep breath, he will breathe with his upper chest, which will noticeably expand up and out. This is contrary to diaphragmic breathing practiced by the kung fu master and prescribed by Chinese medicine. Chuang Tzu, the great Chinese sage, said that men of great wisdom fetch their breath up from deep inside them—common knowlege for thousands of years. Thus in Oriental deep breathing, the diaphragm does all the work, not the chest which scarcely moves at all. Witnessed, the stomach seems to bulge outward as the student inhales and collapses inward as he exhales. This type of breathing has a number of immediate benefits. First, it completely empties the lungs. This is of enormous value because during ordinary unconscious breathing we utilize less than a deep inside them—common knowledge for thousands sands of years. Thus in Oriental deep breathing, the diaphragm does all the work, not the chest which scarcely moves at all. Witnessed, the stomach seems to bulge outward as the student inhales and collapses inward as he exhales. This type of breathing has a number of immediate benefits. First, it completely empties the lungs. This is of enormous value because during ordinary unconscious breathing we utilize less than a quarter of our lung capacity. As a result, we gradually accumulate a great deal of stale air and carbon dioxide in our lungs. This is totally flushed out, and the blood becomes more richly oxygenated. This rich blood, which circulates to all the organs, gives the body a quick pick-me-up—which is soon felt when it reaches the brain. Won't ordinary deep breathing accomplish the same thing? Absolutely not, deep thoracic breathing only empties the lungs partially because it moves only the rib cage, not the diaphragm which is the muscle that controls breathing. Moreover, the diaphragm is strategically placed beneath the lungs, making it better suited to completel; empty and fill the lungs than the auxiliary muscles at the side of the chest. A less immediate benefit, but one that is just as vital, is that all this pronounced diaphragm movement massages all the internal organs in its area including the stomach, liver, reproductive organs, intestines, etc. A massaged organ, according to the Chinese, is a tonified organ and ultimately one that is much stronger.

Chinese medicine has recognized the importance of breathing exercises and medical gymnastics as a cure for a wide variety of ailments. Many modern mainland sanitariums utilize them regularly in treating ulcers, prolapse of the stomach, malignant vomiting, nervous breakdowns, and a wide variety of other problems. The cures documented in hundreds of cases are absolutely extraordinary—ranging from 75 to 100 percent! Chinese physicians further vindicated these age-old methods by measuring the size of various internal organs before the exercises were given, and then measuring them after the treatment was completed. In all cases where the patients were cured there was a marked increase in the size of the internal organs. Strangely enough, the published reports of these studies have been available since 1958, yet western medicine has either dismissed them, as it did acupuncture for centuries, or simply not bothered to study them.

Herbal remedies, another area that the West has long laughed at as silly superstition, have been successfully utilized for thousands of years by kung fu men and Chinese physicians. For example, a report in the *Chinese Medical Journal* in 1957 told of a 99 percent cure rate in a test group of 309 leprosy patients. They were cured in nine months using a traditional prescription containing extracts from thirty medicinal herbs. Similarly, western science only recently discovered that ma huang, or Chinese horsetail which the Chinese have used for thousands of years in treating asthma, actually turned out to contain natural ephedrine—the current western remedy for asthmatic ailments. In another Chinese medical periodical, researchers resurrected an ancient prescription for the treatment of acute bacillary dysentery. The result

—the treatment proved more effective than the use of modern antibiotics such as streptomycin and sulphaguanidine! Further research proved that pien hsu, or prostrate knotweed, the traditional remedy for pulmonary tuberculosis, contained salicylic acid which is exactly what western medicine prescribes for this ailment. These few examples by no means define the extent of Chinese herbal cures. There are literally thousands, many of which Chinese researchers have determined to be more effective than comparable western cures!

The kung fu man's interest in herbal remedies started on a much simpler level than all these advanced discoveries—he needed to know how to care for sprains, bruises, and wounds received in sparring practice or actual combat. While it is uncertain if kung fu men were responsible for actually discovering these remedies, it is known that their rudimentary medical chests first contained pain-killers (Chu-hua, Ma-jen, and Wu-t'ou), antiseptics (P'u-ho and Huang-ch'angshan), restoratives (Hsueh-chieh and Jen-shen), and herbs for treating open sores (Lu-huei and Chih-tzu-mien). In time, as kung fu grew, these early practitioners became increasingly concerned with the health of the total man. It became necessary to acquire additional knowledge until many masters became skilled pharmacologists as well. In the better schools, the master looked after the day-to-day health of his students almost as a matter of course. Various herb teas were given to the students daily as a means of regulating the internal functions of their bodies. Moreover, herbs were prescribed for specific training, particularly when it came to toughening various parts of the body used in striking. In the monasteries, the monks extensively studied the effects of these different herbs. Their experimentation did much to codify what was known, and helped the further spread of knowledge. Some became virtual repositories of herbal recipes which might have been otherwise lost in the periods of turbulence that frequently shook the country.

Massage, moxibustion, and acupuncture while

familiar to the Chinese for years have only recently gained attention in the West. All three are mentioned together because they all function on the same principle—the tonification of the pathways called meridians. These meridians comprise an interlocking system that connects the various internal organs with each other, as well as with the nervous, glandular, and circulatory systems. Unrecognized by western medicine, the physical existence of these pathways has been proved by a Korean biologist who injected a radioactive substance into them and traced its flow. The result—the existence of a separate internal system which functions much like the circulatory system. A section of one of these meridians was removed and then examined under an electron microscope. Two things were found—first, the existence of what Chinese have traditionally called *chi*; second, a fluid containing cells in the process of formation. In addition, on the meridians small structures of excitable tissue were found. These corresponded to the traditional acupuncture points which when stimulated either increase or decrease the flow in the meridian. This flow is directed to the internal organs, glands, and so forth and has either a sedating or tonifying effect. Thus if the liver is not producing enough bile, stimulation of the correct points will jolt the liver into activity. There are three ways to stimulate these points —through rubbing, heating, and needling, Rubbing, or massage, is the gentlest of the three and is often the first used in treatment. Moxibustion, which is lightly heating the points with a burning cone of the herb moxa, is a means of further stimulation if massage is not effective. Acupuncture, which needles the points, is the most extreme (although hardly painful) of the methods. To be familiar with the system is to be able to utilize all three means of treatment.

The kung fu man uses all three in dealing with injuries and health problems. It is impossible to determine when this practice began, but today many of the best kung fu masters are also doctors of acupuncture. As we have discussed, these acupuncture points may also be used for destruction. Hitting discordant parts can damage as well as cure, which is how the art tieh-hsueh originated. Learning acupuncture is a difficult undertaking. It takes years of practice and is one more reason why it takes a lifetime for a kung fu man to become a master.

So ends this quick sketch of Chinese medicine and kung fu. For those who are interested in a more in-depth treatment, my prior book, *The Kung Fu Exercise Book,* should answer many questions.

6

Kung Fu Weaponry

An accurate discussion of kung fu is incomplete without a thorough examination of kung fu weaponry and training. Kung fu men, contrary to popular western belief, did not limit their martial interests solely to hand-to-hand combat. Training in the use of a wide variety of weapons has *always* been required by reputable kung fu schools. The reasons for this mandatory training are as varied as the mosaic of Chinese history. As previously mentioned, early records indicate that weapons proficiency in the army was a virtual necessity for advancement through the ranks, not to mention staying alive. And as every male was expected to serve two years, most men had at least a rudimentary training in arms. Not to have some skill with a weapon meant that the rest of the populace was unlikely to treat you with respect—a dangerous situation in a violent society.

China's long history of lawless epochs further increased the value of weapon training. During these periods, virtual armies of highwaymen and pirates prowled land and sea looking for fat merchant con-

整礪戎器圖

voys or rich peasants to terrorize. These predators were armed to the teeth, and a kung fu man who relied solely on hand techniques was either a great master or a fool. Many kung fu men utilized these hazardous times to their advantage. By hiring out to merchant convoys and villagers alike, they not only made a good living, but were able to keep their skills sharp and test new techniques.

On a more individual level, a master was continually being challenged to maintain his reputation. The reasons behind these challenges were many. Just as in the American West, there was no scarcity of hotheaded young kids out to make a name for themselves. The most serious challenges came from other masters who were eager to prove that their system was superior. If such a man defeated a reigning master, not only would he achieve widespread fame, but he would frequently inherit much of the defeated master's school. As this was often a very lucrative proposition, rivalary and jealousy among kung fu men became commonplace. Because of the high stakes challenges were frequently issued that called for weapons. A kung fu man had to be as proficient with weapons as he was in unarmed combat or face defeat. Since old traditions die hard, such contests were common even as recently as 1920!

Weapons training became even more essential when the Manchus came to power. The new dynasty was using its army to hunt down Ming supporters. Faced with heavily armed troops, the kung fu men of that era built their own armies. Emphasis on weapons training was heavy, as their adversaries were armed with traditional Chinese weapons (guns did not become common until sometime later).

Finally, weapons training became a valuable method of teaching unarmed techniques. Today many schools in the United States do not teach weapons tactics to beginners; yet, some experts insist that kung fu weapons, taught from the beginning, develop strength, timing, speed, control, accuracy, and grace. This makes a great deal of sense as it is widely acknowledged that weapons tactics are merely an extension of the hand. Consequently, this is the way unarmed kung fu techniques have been taught in China for thousands of years. Toward developing weapons proficiency the student is taught lengthy and intricate sets of movements just as in the unarmed forms.

To further demonstrate this point, as well as introduce the reader to some kung fu weapons, here are some of the more popular ones used in teaching the art:

The quando is a long heavy staff with an enormous vicious-looking blade on one end and a deadly point on the other. Its weight and bulk are used to build strength—not a static strength, but a living, moving strength capable of responding to a wide variety of situations. Reputedly, the quando forms develop the body evenly so that no part is ever stronger or out of proportion to another. This is particularly valuable as many kung fu men tend to overdevelop their musculature. For example, the biceps are frequently enlarged at the expense of the elbow sinews which results in students' throwing their elbows out of joint while practicing punches.

Staff techniques develop coordination between the hands and the legs. A hand that is slightly out of place will cause the tip of the staff to be more than one foot off course. Similarly, a leg that is not properly positioned will impede staff movements. In order to complete the complex staff forms successfully, the entire body must work together. Such unity of movement teaches the student how to coordinate the legs and arms through precise, accurate motions—a very valuable skill in unarmed combat.

The double-edged sword is known as the most difficult weapon to master. The student wields the sword in a relaxed manner, gently moving it in small circles with increasing subtlety. Its purpose is to achieve a serene tai chi-like spiritual centering. When properly performed it amounts to a meditative experience, heightening awareness, bringing the student into contact with his inner self.

The double hook axes are exotic-looking weapons

that defy description. Every surface of them is sharp, except where they are gripped. Two axes of this variety are always in tandem while exercising. The student soon becomes aware that an endless variety of techniques is possible as both axes can link up with each other, effectively doubling their range. Though complex and difficult to master, they teach that distance and timing can overcome even the strongest opponent.

Staffs, originally used as a means of carrying heavy burdens, evolved into defensive weapons during one of China's many lawless periods. By balancing a staff on the shoulder, it was possible to carry two heavy baskets of goods. If attacked, however, the baskets could slip from the end of the staff and it would immediately be transformed into a heavy serviceable weapon.

The chain imitates many of the loose hand styles that are prevalent in the north of China. Its whipping action demands a flexible wrist and a good eye for distance. It also teaches the student how to control his momentum or else suffer the consequences of having the chain boomerang with alarming speed and force.

Briefly, some of the other weapons in the kung fu arsenal are:

The three-sectioned staff—strengthens the forearms, wrists, and fingers. Very valuable for the tiger claw school which relies on these parts of the anatomy for striking.

The spear—develops speed. At one time considered the king of weapons, as even the British admitted that it was far superior to their bayonets.

The trident—developed as the ideal weapon for protecting a man from a tiger, it became an excellent defensive device used against other two-legged predatory animals.

The saber—teaches strong chopping motions. A valuable aid as many hand blows are delivered as a chop.

This by no means exhausts the enormous variety of kung fu weaponry. There is the chuean, a four-edged sword; the battle hammer and battle ax; the tsow, a staff with a metal hand at the end of it used to hit nerve and blood centers; the chan, a strange type of blunted staff used mostly by monks; the rake; the hooked spear; and the butterfly knives, usually used in pairs and effective against many larger weapons including the spear. In all, there are more than eighteen weapons that have given birth to more than four hundred complex forms. The reason for this enormous number of forms is that almost every school has its own weapons styles, including the internal schools such as tai chi.

The overwhelming popularity of weapons can be traced to the Chinese cultural giants. Confucius, in 500 B.C., suggested that his followers practice archery. Li Po, the famed poet, wrote that he was "keen on swordplay at fifteen." And Tu Fu, another major poet, was reputedly enormously skilled with a bow and wrote a famous poem celebrating the swordplay of a certain Madame Kung Sun. These associations gave weapons and unarmed combat an aura of culture and refinement that could have only existed in the strange and startling civilization that is China.

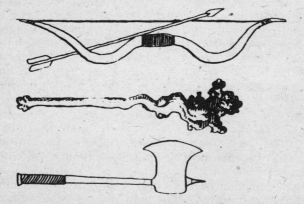

PART 2

The Wisdom of the Masters

For thousands of years Chinese philosophy has been the single most potent force in Chinese history and civilization. It has destroyed empires, established bureaucracies, and instituted moral codes that affected everyone—from the mightiest emperor to the lowliest peasant. Never in the history of civilization have philosophers and sages exerted such enormous influence or wielded so much power and moral authority. In the West, the only institutions that have come close to exercising similar power have been the great religions. A number of superficial similarities have prompted many westerners to perceive the great Chinese philosophies as religions. Nothing could be further from the truth. Confucianism, Taoism, and Buddhism (the most significant of the many Chinese philosophies) are not forms of worship, but unique ways of thinking and seeing the world as well as man's relationship to his fellow man and his own inner nature.

Just how deeply these ways of thought have influenced Chinese civilization is difficult for the western reader to appreciate. Confucius, for example, while unsuccessful during his lifetime, would have been pleased to discover entire governments and states organized and ruled by his principles. But the famous oriental scholar, Wing-Tsit Chan, best summed up this pervasive influence in her description of Taoist philosophy when she said, "No one can hope to understand Chinese philosophy, religion, government, art, medicine—or even cooking—without a real appreciation of the profound philosophy of Lao Tzu [the founding father of Taoism]."

The same applies to the other great Chinese philosophies which are the motivating spirit behind virtually every skill and ability in Chinese culture. Kung fu, naturally, is no exception. The kung fu warrior from the earliest times has been deeply enmeshed in these ways of thinking. To assume that the wisdom and philosophy of the kung fu man was different from that embraced by the rest of Chinese culture would be a grave error. The kung fu man was a product of his culture, and as such, the way he lived mirrored the prevailing thought of his times. *Thus the wisdom of the kung fu masters and the wisdom of the ancient sages are one and the same.* Nor does the relationship between kung fu and the ancient sages and patriarchs stop here. Many of the cultural giants in Chinese history definitely practiced rudimentary forms of kung fu—one only has to read their writings to find frequent references to the early forms of the art. Confucius ordered his students to practice martial arts, specifically archery and charioteering, although some experts believe that they also learned a secret form of unarmed combat. The Buddhist patriarch, Ta Mo, not only brought Zen Buddhism to China, but founded the famed Shaolin branch of the art. Lao Tzu's writings are filled with military advice (then and even now considered part of kung fu) as well as practical advice on how to raise *chi*.

The sages' interest in many aspects of the art greatly encouraged priests and patriarchs of subsequent eras to practice kung fu. Taoist monks, long before the rise of the Shaolin Temple, became expert swordsmen.

成湯圖

And the Buddhists of a later era refined kung fu to a level which has yet to be approached by modern-day masters. Confucians continued to follow the dictates of their founder Kung Fu Tzu (i.e., Confucius whose name came to reflect kung fu), becoming increasingly adept in the martial arts. Consequently, later day kung fu masters were often Taoist, Buddhist, or Confucian sages; and their wisdom and teaching reflected the school of thought that they came from.

To further insure that kung fu men reflected the traditional wisdom of the masters, the serious student was required to study all the Chinese classics, and commit much of them to memory. The works of the Confucian scholars were a particular must, and much of the daily speech of the kung fu man was spotted with sayings, quotes, and advice of these sages. This type of education literally insured that future masters would reflect the wisdom of the ancients, and any new ideas would be a welcome addition to the knowledge that then ruled Chinese society.

This intellectual harmony was just as much a product of the three major philosophies as the above method of schooling. While lesser men quarreled over the different doctrines, wise men saw them as complementary. Confucianism was a plea for humanity in government and personal relationship (something that never existed in China until Confucius first suggested it). Taoism is a mystical approach to life stressing simplicity, spontaneity, tranquillity, and achieving all goals through Non-Striving. Buddhism taught an eightfold path for pure living, and most of its important doctrines have identical counterparts in Taoist thought. Ironically, all three schools have argued bitterly from time to time and even persecuted each other when in power. Hui Hau, the great Buddhist patriarch, saddened by the futility of the constant strife best summed up the real differences between the systems when he said:

"Employed by men of unlimited intellect, they are the same. As understood by men of limited intellect, they differ. All of them spring forth from the functioning of the one self nature. It is views involving diferentiation that makes them three. Whether a man remains deluded or gains illumination depends on himself, not on differences or similarities of doctrine."

In the final analysis, the primary concern of all three great philosophies is spiritual enlightenment. How this is accomplished varies somewhat from school to school; yet all have one thing in common—each approach relies heavily on a wide variety of moral teachings. Thus much of the wisdom of the sages and kung fu masters is advice on Right Living (some of which will sound familiar to western ears) because without a virtuous existence it is possible to understand higher realities and waken internal powers.

The following chapters are the result of a painstaking distillation of the major and minor schools of Chinese thought and proverbial wisdom. More than being required reading for those on the kung fu path, these ideas were embraced by all Chinese who sought higher knowledge. Thus the brief quotation and stories that follow are the heart and soul of the teachings that motivated kung fu masters for thousands of years.

It can be said with total certainty that if these unique ways of thinking had never developed, kung fu would today be little more than a fancy method of pugilism, instead of the rich complex art that it has gradually evolved into. So once again history has demonstrated the enormous power of words and ideas to utterly transform even the simplest discipline. Thus we begin this voyage into the kung fu mind with the words of an ancient anonymous sage who said:

Without ascending the mountain, we cannot judge the height of Heaven.
Without descending into the valley, we cannot judge the depth of the earth.
Without listening to the maxims of the ancient masters, we cannot know the excellence of learning.
The words of saints though a thousand years old do not become useless.

Mysticism

What truly is within will be manifested without.
> —*The Great Learning*

God is within you; you have no doubts in your heart.
> —*She King*

Everything in the past died yesterday; everything in the future was born today.
> —*Anonymous*

If a great ruler were to acknowledge and follow your advice, be perfectly satisfied. If not one should heed your advice, be the same.
> —*Mencius*

Be not like those who are ruled by their passions and desires.
> —*She King*

When thoughts arise, then do all things arise. When thoughts vanish, then do all things vanish.
> —*Huang Po*

The doctrine of the absence of mind is wrong. Instead, we should say only the absence of the selfish mind.
> —*I-ch'uan*

Mind has no color, such as green or yellow, red or white; it is not long or short; it does not vanish or appear; it is free from purity and impurity alike; and its duration is eternal. It is utter stillness.

Such then is the form of our original mind, which is also our original body.
> —*Hui Hai*

Our bodies are the creations of our minds.
> —*Chih Kung*

The great end of learning is nothing else but to seek for the lost mind. —Mencius

The wise not thinking become foolish, and the foolish not thinking become wise. —Shoo King

When men do not forget what should be easily forgotten, and forget what is not easily forgotten . . . we have a case of real oblivion. —Chuang Tzu

As soon as the mouth is open, evils spring forth. People either neglect the root and speak of the branches, or neglect the reality of the "illusionary" world and speak only of Enlightenment. —Huang Po

Fishing baskets are employed to catch fish; but when fish are got, the men forget the baskets. Snares are employed to catch hares; but when the hares are got, men forget the snares. Words are employed to convey ideas; but when the ideas are truly comprehended, men forget the words. Fain would I talk with such a man who has forgotten the words. —Chuang Tzu

When the world, because of the value which it attaches to words, commits them to books, that for which it so values them may not deserve to be valued . . . because that which it values is not what is really valuable. —Chuang Tzu

Stepping into the public hall for a lecture the Master was observed to say:
"Having many sorts of knowledge cannot be compared with giving up *seeking* for anything, which is the best of all things. Mind is not of several kinds and there is no Doctrine which can be put into words. As there is no more to be said, the assembly is dismissed." —Huang Po

Ultimate realization means being free from both realization and absence of realization. —Hui Hai

顛木由蘖圖

Those who dream of the pleasures of drinking may in the morning wail and weep. Those who dream of wailing and weeping may in the morning be going out to hunt. When they are dreaming they did not know it was a dream; but when they awoke they knew it was a dream.

Thus it is said that there is the Great Awakening, after which we shall know that this life was a great dream, while all the while the stupid think that they are awake.   —*Chuang Tzu*

The Sage-like man knows the way of what the ancients called The Heavenly Treasure House. He may pour into it without its being filled; he may pour from it without being exhausted; and all the time he does not know from whence the supply comes.
                                    —*Chuang Tzu*

To be *at will* either bright or obscure, soft or hard, short or long, round or square, sweet or bitter, present or absent, alive or dead . . . this is to be devoid of knowledge, yet all-knowing, destitute of power, yet all-powerful.   —*Lieh Tzu*

That which fills the universe I regard as my body and that which directs the universe I consider as my nature.   —*Chang Tsai*

If you discriminate between today and tomorrow, that is like using your own true nature to search for your own true nature; you will not perceive it even after thousands of aeons. Yours would then be the case of not seeing the sun, not of there being no sun.   —*Hui Hau*

To mistake material surroundings for True Reality is to mistake a thief for your son.   —*Huang Po*

He who understands the conditions of life does not strive after what is no use to life; and he who understands the conditions of destiny does not strive after what is beyond the reach of knowledge. —*Chuang Tzu*

Remember that from first to last not even the smallest grain of anything perceptible has ever existed or will ever exist.   —*Chuang Tzu*

The perfect man leaves no traces of his conduct.
                                        —*Chuang Tzu*

Calamity and happiness . . . in all cases they are men's own seeking.   —*Mencius*

Joy and anger, sadness and pleasure, anticipation and regret, eagerness and tardiness, vehemence and indolence, fickleness and fixedness . . . are but emotional moods which like music from an empty tube, or mushrooms from the warm moisture endlessly succeed one and another . . .   —*Chuang Tzu*

Pleasure when past is converted to pain.
                                        —*Anonymous*

What was anciently called "the Attainment of the Aim" did not mean the getting of carriages and coronets (worldly distinction); it simply meant that nothing more was needed for their enjoyment. Nowadays what is called "the Attainment of the Aim" means the getting of carriages and coronets. But carriages and coronets belong solely to the material world. When such things happen to come to a man, it is but for a time; being but for a time, their coming cannot be obstructed and their going cannot be stopped. If now the departure of what is transient takes away one's enjoyment, this demonstrates that what enjoyment it had given was worthless.

Hence it is said, "They who lose themselves in their pursuit of material objects, and lose their nature in the study of what is vulgar, must be pronounced people who turn things upside-down."   —*Chuang Tzu*

Nirvana is a deep sea of wisdom; the material universe is but a whirling chaos.   —*Huang Po*

What men consider bitter experiences are that their

bodies do not get rest and ease, that their mouths do not get food of rich flavor, that their persons are not finely clothed, that their eyes do not see beautiful colors, and that their ears do not listen to pleasant music. If they do not get these things they are very sorrowful, and go on to be troubled with fears. Their thoughts are all about the body and the material world—are they not silly?   —Chuang Tzu

When aroused become awake; when awake reach Understanding.   —Anonymous

Meditation in activity is a hundred, a thousand, a million times superior to meditation in repose.
               —Anonymous

To nourish the heart there is nothing better than to make the desires few . . .   —Mencius

Some madman shrieking on the mountaintop, on hearing the echo far below, may go to seek it in the valley. Once in the valley, he shrieks again and straightway climbs to search back among the peaks. Such a man may spend a thousand rebirths searching for the source of these sounds by following their echoes. Far better that you make no sound, for then there will be no echo and you will be one with the dwellers in Nirvana.   —Huang Po

If you pursue knowledge for a thousand days, that will avail you less than one day's proper study of the true workings of the mind. If you do not study it, you will be unable to digest even a single drop of water.   —Huang Po

Wisdom is not without its perils, and spirit-like intelligence does not reach to everything. A man may have the greatest wisdom, but there still may be many men scheming against him. Put away your small wisdom, and your great wisdom will become bright; discard your skillfulness, and you will become naturally skillful. A child when it is born needs no great master, and yet it becomes able to speak, living as it does among those who are able to speak.　　　*—Chuang Tzu*

He who devotes himself to learning seeks from day to day to increase his knowlege. He who devotes himself to knowing his true nature seeks from day to day to diminish his doing.　　　*—Lao Tzu*

The greatest politeness is to show no special respect to others; the greatest righteousness is to take no account of things; the greatest wisdom is to lay no plans; the greatest benevolence is to make no unseemly display of affection; the greatest good faith is to give no pledge of sincerity.　　　*—Chuang Tzu*

The mountain by its trees weakens itself. The grease which ministers to the fire fries itself. The cinnamon tree can be eaten, and therefore it is cut down. The varnish tree is useful, and therefore incisions are made in it. All men know the advantage of being useful, but no one knows the advantage of being useless.
　　　—Khieh-yu, the madman of Khu

Huang Ti, enjoying himself on the north of the Red-water, was returning home when he lost his dark-colored pearl. He employed Wisdom to search for it, but he could not find it. He employed the clear-sighted Li Ku to search for it, but he could not find it. He employed the vehement debater Khieh Khau to search for it, but he could not find it. Finally he employed Purposeless, who found it; on which Huang Ti said, "How strange that it was Purposeless who was able to find it!"　　　*—Chuang Tzu*

A man who does little more than eat and drink is counted as common by others—because he nourishes what is little to the neglect of what is great.　*—Mencius*

To preserve one's mental and physical constitution and *nourish one's nature* is the way to serve Heaven.
　　　—Mencius

It is most difficult for love to last long; therefore who loves passionately is in the end cured of love. Human nature is eternal; therefore who follows his nature in the end retains his original nature. —Tut-Tut

To be elated at success and disappointed at failure is to be the child of circumstances; how can such a one be called the master of himself? —Tut-Tut

Honors and riches, distinctions and austerity, fame and profit—these six things produce the impulses of the will.

Personal appearance and deportment, the desire of beauty and subtle reasoning, excitement of the breath and cherished thoughts—these six things produce the errors of the mind.

Hatred and longings, joy and anger, grief and delight—these six things are the entanglements of virtue.

Refusals and reproachments, receiving and giving, knowledge and ability—these six things obstruct the way of the sagely minded man.

When these four conditions, with their six causes

each, do not agitate the breast, the mind is correct. Being correct, it is still; being still, it is pellucid; being pellucid, it is free from preoccupation; being free from preoccupation, it is in a state of inaction, in which it accomplishes everything. —*Chuang Tzu*

The *Way* is through Mind-awakening, and it cannot be conveyed through words. Speech only produces some effect when it falls on the uninstructed ears of children. —*Huang Po*

If a man is crossing a river in a boat and another empty vessel collides with it, even a man with a hot temper will not become angry. But it there be a helmsman in the boat, the hot-tempered man will break into a rage and become abusive.

Formerly he was not angry, but now he is; formerly he thought the boat empty, but now there is a person in it. If a man can empty himself of thoughts of himself, who can harm him during his time in this world? —*Chuang Tzu*

He who works for eternity counts not time. —*Anonymous*

He who knows spiritual wisdom has no need to speak about it; he who is ever ready to speak about it does not know it. —*Lao Tzu*

A sage speaks for the universe. —*Chang Chao*

When I pronounce men to be quick of hearing, I do not mean that they harken to anything else, but that they harken to themselves.

When I pronounced them to be clear of vision, I do not mean that they look to anything else, but that they look to themselves. —*Chuang Tzu*

The Sixth Patriarch while talking to the elder Wei Ming said: "Perhaps you will concentrate your thoughts for a moment and avoid thinking in terms of good and evil."

Ming did as he was told, and the Sixth Patriarch continued: "While you are not thinking of good and not thinking of evil, just at this moment, return to what you were before your father and mother were born."

Even as the words were spoken, Ming received sudden illumination.   —Huang Po

To him who has what is most noble, all the dignities of a state are as nothing; to him who has what are the greatest riches, all the wealth of a state is as nothing; to him who has all that he could wish, fame and praise are as nothing.   —Chuang Tzu

Chuang Tzu was fishing in the river Phu when the king of Khu sent two high officers to him with the message, "I wish to trouble you with the charge of all within my territories."

Chuang Tzu kept holding his rod without looking around and said, "I have heard that in Khu there is a magnificent tortoiseshell, the wearer of which died three thousand years ago, and which the king keeps in his ancestral temple. Was it better for the tortoise to die, and leave its shell to be thus honored? Or would it have been better for it to live, and drag its tail after it over the mud?"

The two officers replied, "It would have been better for it to live, and drag its tail after it through the mud."

"Go your way," said Chuang Tzu, "I will keep on dragging my tail after me through the mud."

                                    —Chuang Tzu

The great man is he who does not lose his child's heart.   —Mencius

Public spirited, and with nothing of the partisan; easy and compliant; without any selfish tendencies; following in the wake of others, without a double mind; not easily distracted because of any anxious thoughts; not scheming in the exercise of one's wisdom; not choosing between parties, but going along

with all—all such courses are the paths to true enlightenment.
—*Chuang Tzu*

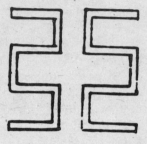

In God's eyes, there is no rejected person. —*Lao Tzu*

One without a pitying heart is not a man.
One without a merciful heart is not a Buddha.
—*Anonymous*

Buddha is on the efficacious mountain, so do not seek him at a distance; the efficacious mountain is on the apex of the heart, so every man has a pagoda on it; it is truly good to cultivate the space at the base of the pagoda.
—*Anonymous*

Not to be separate from the primal source constitutes what we call the Heavenly man; not to be separate from the essential nature thereof constitutes what we call the Spirit-like man; not be separate from its real truth constitutes what we call the Perfect man.
—*Chuang Tzu*

Without going outside one's door it is possible to

understand all that takes place under the sky.

Without looking out one's window it is possible to obtain the kingdom of Heaven.

The further one goes from himself, the less he knows.

Thus the ancient sages got their knowledge without traveling; gave the right names to things without seeing them; and accomplished their ends without any purpose of doing so.   —*Lao Tzu*

Man comes forth, but from no root; he reenters, but by no aperture. He has real existence, but it has nothing to do with place. He has continuance, but it has nothing to do with beginning or end. Such is man's relation to the material world. Man has life; he has death; he comes forth; he enters; we do not see his form—all this is called the door of Heaven.

     —*Chuang Tzu*

To see through fame and wealth is to gain a little rest; to see through life and death is to gain a big rest.   —*Tut-Tut*

The door of Heaven is Non-Existence. All things come from Non-Existence. The first existences could but bring themselves into Existence; thus they must have come from Non-Existence. And Non-Existence is just the same as not existing. Herein is the secret of the sages.   —*Chuang Tzu*

The source of life is death, but that which produces life never comes to an end. The origin of form is matter, but that which imparts form has no material existence. The genesis of sound lies in the sense of hearing, but that which causes sound is never audible to the ear. The source of color is vision, but that which produces color never manifests itself to the eye. The origin of taste lies in the palate, but that which causes taste is never perceived by that sense.   —*Lieh Tzu*

All things come from somewhere, but you cannot

see their root; all things appear from somewhere, but you cannot see the door.   —*Chuang Tzu*

That which has life returns again to the Lifeless; that which has substance returns again to the Insubstantial. The course of evolution ends where it started, without a beginning; it finishes up where it began, in Not-Being.   —*Lieh Tzu*

Just as surely as water overcomes the greatest rocks, so does the weak overcome the strong.

He who knows other men is intelligent, while he who overcomes himself is truly wise.

He who overcomes others is strong, while he who overcomes himself knows true power.

He who accumulates wealth for its own sake is a poor man, while he who is satisfied with his lot has a life of riches.

He who learns not his true nature knows death. He who has touched his own soul dies yet does not perish.   —*Lao Tzu*

One day Kwang Kau fell into a deep sleep and dreamed that he was a butterfly sailing over the countryside.

Suddenly Kau awoke finding himself in his own body. After a moment's reflection he knew not if he was Kau dreaming that he was a butterfly, or if he was a butterfly now dreaming that he was Kau.

—*Chuang Tzu*

Kung-ni when asked to deliver a toast to the king of Khu responded thusly,

"I have heard of a speech without words; but I have never spoken it; I will do so now. I-liao of Shih-nan quietly handled two brass spheres and the difficulties between two warring houses were resolved. Sun Shu-ao slept undisturbed with a feather in his hand, and the men of Ying enrolled themselves for war. I wish I had a beak three cubits long."   —*Chuang Tzu*

Yao, the wise man, was looking around at Hwa

when he was approached by the border-warden who said, "Ha! the sage! Let me ask blessings on the sage! May he live long!"

Yao said, 'Hush!' but the other went on, "May the sage become rich!"

Yao again said, "Hush!"

But the warden continued, "May the sage have many sons!"

When Yao repeated his "Hush!" the warden said, "Long life, riches, and many sons are what men wish for . . . How is it that you alone do not wish for them?"

Yao replied, "Many sons bring many fears; riches bring many troubles; and long life gives rise to slander."

—*Chuang Tzu*

He who has reached the stage of thought is silent.

He who has attained perfect knowledge is also silent.

He who uses silence in lieu of speech really does speak.

He who for knowledge substitutes blankness of mind really does know. Without words and speaking not, without knowledge and knowing not, he really speaks and really knows.

Saying nothing and knowing nothing, there is in reality nothing that he does not say, nothing that he does not know. This is how the matter stands; there is nothing more to be said.

—*Lieh Tzu*

Superior Man

The superior man is distressed by his want of ability; he is not distressed by men's not knowing him.

—*Confucius*

As to what the superior man would feel to be a calamity there is no such thing. He does nothing which is not according to propriety. If there should befall him one morning's calamity, the superior man does not perceive it as such.   —Mencius

In the seventh and eighth months when the rain falls abundantly the channels in the fields are all filled, but their being dried up again may be expected in a short time. So a superior man is ashamed of a reputation that goes beyond his merits.   —Mencius

Tzu-Kung asked what constituted the superior man. The Master said, "He acts before he speaks, and afterward speaks according to his actions."
                                            —Confucius

In archery we have something of the superior man. When the archer misses the center of the target, he turns around and seeks for the cause of his failure in himself.   —Doctrine of the Mean

The superior man wishes to be slow in his words and earnest in his conduct.   —Confucius

That whereby man differs from the lower animals is but small. The mass of people cast it away, while superior men preserve it.   —Mencius

A vulgar man always looks for favors and forgets them when he has got what he wants. A superior man hesitates a great deal before he accepts a favor and then he always remembers it.   —Chen Chiju

The superior man has a dignified ease without pride. The common man has pride without dignified ease.   —Confucius

It is said that the superior man has two things in which he delights, and to be ruler over the empire is not one of them.

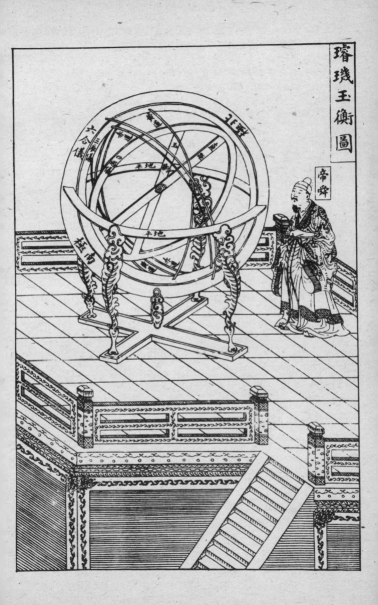

That the father and mother are both alive and that the condition of his brothers affords no cause for anxiety, this is one delight.

That when looking up he has no occasion for shame before Heaven, and below he has no occasion to blush before men—this is the second delight.

—*Mencius*

The superior man hoards nothing.

The more he uses for the benefit of others, the more he possesses himself. The more he gives to his fellow man, the more he has of his own.

—*Lao Tzu*

What the superior man seeks in himself the common man seeks in others. —*Confucius*

The superior man is quiet and calm, awaiting for the appointments of Heaven, while the common man walks in dangerous paths looking for lucky occurrences. —*Doctrine of the Mean*

The superior man loves his soul; the inferior man loves his property. The superior man always remembers how he was punished for his mistakes; the inferior man always remembers what presents he got. —*Confucius*

The superior man understands what is right; the inferior man understands what will sell. —*Confucius*

The skillful traveler leaves no trace of his wheels or footsteps.

The skillful speaker says nothing that can be found fault with.

The skillful reckoner uses no tallies

The skillful locksmith needs no bolts or bars, while to open what he has shut is impossible.

The skillful binder uses no strings or knots, while to unloosen what he has bound is impossible.

In the same way the superior man is skillful in

dealing with men, and so does not cast away anyone
from his doorway.   —Lao Tzu

When the perfect man employs his mind, it is a
mirror. It conducts nothing and anticipates nothing; it
responds to what is before it, but does not dwell on
what is before it. Thus he is able to deal successfully
with all things and injures none.   —Chuang Tzu

The way which the superior man pursues reaches
wide and far and yet is secret.   —Doctrine of the Mean

The superior man's actions may fill all under
Heaven and yet no dissatisfaction or dislike will be
awakened by them.   —The Hsiao King

So is the superior man affected toward animals,
that, having seen them alive he cannot bear to see
them die; having heard their dying cries, he cannot
bear to eat their flesh. Therefore he keeps away from
his cook room.   —Mencius

The superior man prizes three things. The first is
gentleness, the second is frugality, the third is humility. By being gentle he can be bold; by being frugal, he
can be liberal, and by being humble he becomes a
leader among men.   —Lao Tzu

The superior man undergoes three changes.
Looked at from a distance, he appears stern.
When approached, he is mild.
When he is heard to speak, his language is firm and
decided.   —Confucius

There is nothing more visible than what is secret,
and nothing more manifest than what is minute;
therefore, the superior man is watchful over himself
even when alone.   —Doctrine of the Mean

The superior man is like a tool that cuts no one
with its angles, like a corner which injures no one with
its sharpness.

He is straightforward, but allows himself no license; he is bright, but does not dazzle. —*Lao Tzu*

The superior man is firm but does not fight; he mixes easily with others but does not form cliques.
—*Confucius*

The superior man anticipates tasks that are difficult while they are still easy, and does things that would become great while they are small. Therefore, the superior man, while he never does what is great, is able on that account to accomplish the greatest of things. —*Lao Tzu*

The superior man observes the issues in order to know the origin, scrutinizes the past in order to know the future. Such is the principle whereby he attains foreknowledge. —*Lieh Tzu*

There are three things which the superior man guards against.
In youth when the physical powers are not settled, he guards against lust.
When he is strong and the physical powers are full of vigor he guards against quarrelsomeness.
When he is old and the animal powers have decayed, he guards against covetousness. —*Confucius*

You may do good without thinking about fame, but fame will come to you nevertheless.
You may have fame without aiming at riches, but riches are sure to follow in its wake.
You may be rich without wishing to provoke emulation and strife, yet emulation and strife will certainly result.
Hence the superior man is very cautious about how he does good. —*Lieh Tuz*

In view of a superior man as to the ways by which men seek for riches, honors, gain, and advancement, there are few of their wives who would not be

ashamed and weep together on account of them.
—*Mencius*

The superior man diminishes his actions and diminishes them again until he arrives at doing nothing on purpose.

Having arrived at this point of nonaction, there is nothing that he does not do.   —*Lao Tzu*

The perfect man thinks not of himself, the spirit-like man has no thoughts of merit, and the sagely minded man no thoughts of fame.   —*Chuang Tzu*

It is said that the life of a sage is like the action of Heaven.

He does not take the initiative in producing either happiness or calamity.

He responds to the influence acting on him and moves as he feels the pressure.

He rises to act only when he feels the pressure.

He discards wisdom and the memories of the past.

Thus his life seems to float along, and his death seems but a resting.   —*Chuang Tzu*

The man of perfect faith can extend his influence to inanimate things and disembodied spirits; he can move Heaven and earth, and fly to the six cardinal points without encountering any obstacles. —*Lieh Tzu*

He who is skillfull in managing the life entrusted to him travels on the land without fear of the rhinoceros or tiger, and in self-defense need not concern himself with sharp weapons. For the rhinoceros finds no place in him to thrust its horn, nor the tiger a place in which to fix its claws, nor the weapon a place to admit its point.

And for what reason? Because there is in him no place of death.   —*Lao Tzu*

To keep from being entangled by prevailing customs; to shun all ornamental attractions in oneself; not to be reckless in his conduct with others; to set himself stubbornly against a multitude; to desire the peace and repose of the world in order to preserve the lives of people; and to cease his action when enough has been obtained for the nourishment of others and himself, showing that this was the aim of his mind—such are the ways of the superior man. —*Chuang Tzu*

The wise man treasures what other men consider trash, does not prize things that are difficult to get; turns back to study what other men have passed by.

Such a man acting within the harmony of nature finds true peace where others find chaos.
—*Lao Tzu*

Though the white gem be cast into the dirt, its purity cannot long be sullied; though the good man live in a vile place, his heart cannot be depraved. As the fir and the cypress withstand the rigors of winter, so resplendent wisdom is safe in situations of difficulty and danger. —*Anonymous*

Riches are what a man of worth considers lightly; death is what the ordinary man deems of importance.
—*Anonymous*

He who is concerned about the highest virtue is not in harmony with popular ideas; he who accomplishes a great work frequently does not take counsel with the multitudes. —*Kuo Yen*

If the superior man abandons virtue, how can he fulfill the requirements of that name? —*Confucius*

A man of humanity is a man of both altruism and love.

Altruism is the application of humanity, while love is its function. —*Chu Hsi*

The mistakes of a great and good man are like the eclipses of the sun and moon; his failing is seen by all, and when he repairs it, all look to him with awe.
—*Tzu Kung*

A miser can amass a considerable fortune, but let something happen and he will be like a crushed rat on the streets.

A big-hearted man can also go broke, but something happens and he stays alive as a centipede who has lost some legs.

—*Shu Shuehmou*

The wise man, after learning something new, is afraid to learn anything more until he has put his first lesson into practice.

—*Tzu Lu*

The wise man acts without thinking of acting, tastes without discerning any flavor, sees the few as many, considers what is small as great, experiences sorrow but is not troubled. Thus, while the wise man never does what others consider great, he is able to accomplish the greatest of things.

—*Lao Tzu*

The wise man puts his trust in others; thus he reaches fullness of years without decay, perfection of wisdom without bewilderment.

—*Lieh Tzu*

Personal talent coupled with a slow temper becomes great talent; wisdom coupled with a pacifist mind becomes true wisdom.

—*Tut-Tut*

Existence gives birth to the notion of nonexistence.
Difficulty produces the concept of ease.

The idea of height and depth arise from the contrast of one with the other.

Therefore the wise man seeks to avoid such polarities by managing his daily affairs without doing anything, by issuing orders without the use of speech.

—*Lao Tzu*

A wise man creates law, but a foolish man is controlled by them; a man of talent performs ceremonies, but a common man is enslaved by them.

With a man who is enslaved by ceremonies, it is not worthwhile to speak about such matters; with a man who is controlled by laws, it is not worthwhile to discuss reform. —*Lord Shang*

The wise man is free from self-display, and therefore he shines.

Free from self-assertion and thereby he is distinguished.

Free from self-boasting, his merit is widely acknowledged.

Free from self-complacency, he ascends the ladder of superiority.

It is because he is thus free from striving that no one in the world is able to strive with him. —*Lao Tzu*

The wise man put personal gain last and thereby is found in the highest places. He recognizes that his body is merely a shell, and thereby his person is preserved. Such a man has no private or personal ends; thereby all his goals (acts) bear fruit. —*Lao Tzu*

The sage-minded man lives a life free from care.

He does not indulge any anxious doubts; he does not lay plans beforehand.

His light is without display; his good faith is without previous arrangment.

His sleep is untroubled by dreams; his waking is followed by no sorrows.

His spirit is guileless and pure; his soul is not subject to weariness.

Vacant and without self-assertion, placid and indifferent, he agrees with the virtues of Heaven.

—*Chuang Tzu*

Words said in anger settle no dispute. Benevolence that flaunts its purity accomplishes nothing.

Courage born of stubborness is meaningless. Thus knowledge that stops at what it knows is greatest. Thus the sage man knows the argument that needs no words and the path that is not trodden. —*Chuang Tzu*

The perfect man is spirit-like.

Great lakes might be boiling around him, yet he would not feel the heat; the Ho and the Han might be frozen up, and he would not feel the cold; thunderbolts may split the mountains and the wind shake the sea but he will remain unafraid.

Neither death nor life changes him; such a being he mounts the clouds, rides the sun and moon, and rambles at ease beyond the four seas. —*Nieh Ch'ueh*

Moral Teachings

No medicine can procure long life, even to the ministers of the emperor; no money can purchase for any man a virtuous posterity. —*Anonymous*

Fine words an an insinuating appearance are seldom associated with virtue. —*Confucius*

Yang-tze, on his way to the city of Sung, passed the night in a lodging house. The master of the house had two concubines—one beautiful and the other ugly.

Yang-tze noticed that the ugly one was honored and admired, while the beautiful one was criticized and looked down upon. When Yang-tze asked the reason a little boy of the house replied, "The beauty knows her beauty and we do not recognize it. The ugly one knows her ugliness, and we do not recognize it." When Yang-tze returned to his disciples he told the story of the two concubines and said, "Remember! Act virtuously, and put away the practice of priding yourself on your virtue. If you do this, where can you go that you will not be loved?"
—*Chuang Tzu*

Riches adorn a house and virtue adorns the person.
—*The Great Learning*

Virtue is not left to stand alone. He who practices it will have neighbors.

Speak of men's virtues as if they were your own, and of their vices as if you were liable to their punishment.

Just as a bad year cannot bring death to the man whose stores of grain are large so an age of corruption cannot confound him whose equipment of virtue is complete.
—*Mencius*

He whose virtue exceeds his talents is a good man.
He whose talents exceed his virtue is an inferior man.
—*Anonymous*

Do not consider any vice as trivial and therefore practice it.
Do not consider any virtue as unimportant and therefore neglect it.
—*Anonymous*

Specious words confound virtue.
Want of forbearance in small matters confounds great plans.
—*Confucius*

Forming resentments with mankind may be called "planting misery."
Putting aside virtuous deeds, instead of practicing, may be called "robbing oneself."
—*Anonymous*

One who does not make good or virtuous causes, but with labor covets wealth and profit, such a one should know that throughout the world gold, silver, and precious things are only loaned one to foolishly look upon for a few years. —Anonymous

Virtue is more to a man than either fire or water.
I have seen men die from treading on fire or water, but I have never seen a man die from treading the course of virtue. —Confucius

It is a little thing to starve to death, but it is a serious matter to lose one's virtue. —Anonymous

Early or late, always be earnest. If you do not attend zealously to your small actions, the result will be to affect your virtue in great matters. —Shoo King

The man who, in view of gain, thinks of righteousness; who, in the view of danger, is prepared to give up his life; and who does not forget an old agreement, however far back in extends—such a man may be reckoned a complete man. —Confucius

Benevolence is man's mind and righteous is man's path.
How lamentable it is to neglect the path and not pursue it, to lose the mind and not know to seek it again. —Mencius

Benevolence is the characteristic element of humanity and the great exercise of it is in loving relatives.
Righteousness is the accordance of actions with what is right, and the great exercise of it is in honoring the worthy. —Doctrine of the Mean

There are those who hate death and ruin, yet delight in not being benevolent; this is like hating to be drunk but not being strong enough to put aside wine.
—Mencius

Benevolence subdues its opposite just as water subdues fire.

Those, however, who nowadays practice benevolence do it as if with one cup of water they could save a whole wagonload of fuel which was on fire, and, when the flames were not extinguished, were to say that water cannot subdue fire. This conduct greatly encourages those who are not benevolent. —*Mencius*

Men must be decided on what they will not do, and then they are able to act with vigor on what they ought. —*Mencius*

What I do not wish men to do to me I also wish not to do to men. —*Confucius*

Never do what you wouldn't have known. —*Anonymous*

To see what is right and not to do it is to want of courage. —*Confucius*

When you do a favor, do not expect a reward; should you expect a reward, it is not a favor. —*Anonymous*

Better to do a kindness near home than to journey a thousand miles on a religious pilgrimage. —*Anonymous*

It is far better to save one life than to build a seven-story pagoda. —*Anonymous*

After burning paper money (as a sacrifice) there remains but a handful of ashes.

After offering a libation of wine, there is just a little moisture.

These acts are not equal to providing the living with a little to eat. —*Anonymous*

In our actions, we should accord with the will of

懸官懸賞圖

Heaven; in our words, we should consult the feelings of men.
—*Anonymous*

It is impossible to please men in all things; our only care should be to satisfy our own consciences.
—*Anonymous*

I will not be afflicted at men's not knowing me.
I will be afflicted that I do not know men.
—*Confucius*

Be firm in your acts, but easy in your heart; be strict with yourself, but be gentle with your fellow men.
—*Tut-Tut*

Show forbearance and gentleness in teaching others and do not revenge unreasonable conduct.
—*Doctrine of the Mean*

A few kind words do not enter so deeply into a man as an established reputation for kindness. —*Mencius*

He who thinks his great achievements poor shall find his vigor long endures.
—*Lao Tzu*

The fame of men's good action seldom goes beyond their own doors, but their evil deeds are known a thousand miles distant.
—*Anonymous*

Good words shall gain your honor in the marketplace, but good deeds shall gain you friends among men.
—*Lao Tzu*

It is better to believe that a man possess good qualities than to assert that he does not. —*Anonymous*

The length of the Yellow River has a bed hundreds of thousands of feet long, but man's heart has no bottom.
—*Anonymous*

There is no greater delight than to be conscious of sincerity on self-examination. —*Mencius*

There are three questions that the wise man asks himself at the end of each day. They are:

"Have I been conscientious in working with others? Have I been truthful with all who have crossed my path? Have I practiced what I preach?"   —*Tseng Tzu*

If on self-examination I find that I am not upright, shall I not be in fear even of a poor man in loose garments of hair cloth?

If on self-examination I find that I am upright, neither thousands nor tens of thousands will stand in my path.   —*Mencius*

If a man should love others and the emotion is not returned, let him turn inward and examine his own benevolence.

If a man is trying to rule others, and his government is unsuccessful, let him turn inward and examine his wisdom.

If he treats others politely and they do not return the politeness, let him turn inward and examine his own feelings of respect.   —*Mencius*

When we do not by what we do realize what we desire we must turn inward and examine ourselves in every point. When a man's person is correct, the whole empire will turn to him with recognition and submission.   —*Mencius*

When you hear words against which your mind sets itself, you must inquire whether they be not right; when you hear words which accord with your own mind, you must inquire whether they be not contrary to what is right. Oh, what attainment can be made without anxious thought? What achievement can be made without earnest effort?   —*Shoo King*

Though a man may be utterly stupid, he is very perspicacious when reprehending the bad actions of others; though he may be very intelligent, he is dull enough while excusing his own faults.

Do you only correct yourself on the same principles

that you correct others, and excuse others on the same principle that you excuse yourself? —*Anonymous*

The sense of shame is to a man of great importance.
—*Mencius*

A man may not be without shame. When one is ashamed of having been without shame he will afterward not have occasion for shame. —*Mencius*

When one differs from other men in not having a sense of shame, what will he have in common with them? —*Mencius*

Looked at in friendly intercourse with superior men, you make your countenance harmonious and mild, anxious not to do anything wrong.
Looked at in your chamber, you ought to be equally free from shame before the light which shines in.
Do not say, this place is not public; no one can see me here . . . . —*She King*

Deal with evil as if it were a sickness in your person.
—*Shoo King*

Do right and do it alone.
Commit something wrong and you will need a gang to work with.
That is why even a burglar posts someone to watch for him. —*Shu Shuehmou*

Between yes and yea, how small the difference!
Between good and evil, how great the difference!
—*Lao Tzu*

If a man be not enlightened within, what lamp shall he light?
If his intentions are not honorable, what prayers shall he repeat? —*Anonymous*

To associate with evil men is like sleeping in the

midst of knives and swords; although you have not been wounded, you are constantly afraid.

—*Anonymous*

He who knows, yet thinks that he does not know, has great wisdom.

He who does not know and thinks he knows is diseased.

—*Lao Tzu*

The mischiefs of fire, or water, or robbers extend only to the body, but those of pernicious doctrines, to the mind.

—*Anonymous*

A man can enlarge the principles which he follows; those principles do not enlarge the man.

—*Confucius*

I have not heard of one's principles being dependent for their manifestation on other men.

—*Mencius*

If one does not serve his parents so as to make them pleased, one will not be trusted by his neighbors.

—*Mencius*

Tsze Chang asked how a man might conduct himself so as to be appreciated everywhere. The Master said:

"Let his words be sincere and truthful and his actions honorable and careful—such conduct may be practiced among the rude tribes of the South and North. If his words be not sincere and truthful and his actions not honorable and careful, will he with such conduct be appreciated even in his own neighborhood?"

—*Confucius*

If speech is sweet, the echo will be sweet; if speech is harsh, the echo will be harsh.

If the body is long the shadow will be long; if the body is short the shadow will be short.

Reputation is only an echo, external conduct only a shadow.

—*Lieh Tzu*

The Master said,
"With coarse rice to eat, with water to drink, and my bended arm for a pillow—I have quiet joy in the midst of these things. Riches and honors acquired by unrighteous are to me as a floating cloud."   —Confucius

To take to oneself unrighteous wealth is like satisfying one's hunger with putrid food, or one's thirst with poisoned wine. It gives temporary relief, but death always follows it.   —Chuang Tzu

There is no guilt greater than to sanction unbridled ambition.
No calamity greater than to be dissatisfied with one's lot.
No fault greater than the wish to wish continually of receiving.   —Lao Tzu

Accumulate learning as you would accumulate wealth; seek moral goodness as you would seek official rank and honor; love your parents as you would your wife and children; look after the country as you would look after your own business affairs. —Tut-Tut

Do you not know of the fate of the praying mantis? It angrily stretches out its arms to arrest the progress of the carriage, unconscious of its inability for such a task, but showing how much it thinks of its own powers.
Be on your guard; be careful. If you cherish a boastful confidence in your own excellence and place yourself in a collision course with another, you are likely to incur the fate of the mantis.   —Chuang Tzu

He who stands on his tiptoes does not stand firm.
He who stretches his legs does not walk easily.
Thus he who displays himself does not shine.
He who vaunts himself does not find his merit acknowledged.
He who is self-conceited has no superiority allowed him.   —Lao Tzu

If a man has read a great number of books and doesn't think things through, he's only a bookcase. One may read through the entire Buddhist Tripitaka, but if he has not a pure heart, he can end up only as a wooden figure.　　　　　　　　　　*—Shu Shuehmou*

With the faithful I would keep faith; with the unfaithful I would also keep faith, in order that they may become faithful.　　　　　　　　　　*—Lao Tzu*

Hold faithfulness and sincerity as first principles.
Have no friends not equal to yourself.
When you have faults, do not fear to abandon them.
　　　　　　　　　　—Confucius

The less indulgence one has for oneself, the more one may have for others.
　　　　—Inscription in the examination hall of Canton

To suffer an insult from those one fears is not true patience; to suffer an insult from those one does not fear is true patience.　　　　　　　　*—Tut-Tut*

He who injures others injures himself.
　　　　　　　　　　—Anonymous

Do not consider yourself so enlarged as to deem others small in comparison.　　　　　*—Shoo King*

Prejudice springs from the dislike of the unlike.
　　　　　　　　　　—Anonymous

The ability to perceive the significance of the small things of the world is the secret of clear sightedness; the guarding of what is soft and vulnerable is the secret of strength.　　　　　　　　*—Lao Tzu*

They who know the truth (or learning) are not equal to those who love it, and they who love it are not equal to those who delight in it.　　　　　*—Confucius*

There is no greater lie than the lie that becomes necessary to defend another lie.   —*Anonymous*

Better to be upright in poverty than depraved in abundance.   —*Anonymous*

Do not vary your promise for any price.
          —*Anonymous*

A gentleman blames himself, while a common man blames others.   —*Confucius*

Show reverence for the weak.   —*Shoo King*

Lambs have the grace to suckle while kneeling, and young crows return part of their food to their parents.
          —*Anonymous*

Never has there been one possessed of complete sincerity who did not move others. Never has there been one who had not sincerity who was able to move others.   —*Mencius*

Lust is a wicked knife that cuts clear into the bones.
          —*Anonymous*

Dogs have more good in them than men think they themselves possess.   —*Anonymous*

I like life indeed, but there is that which I like more than life, and, therefore, I will not seek to possess it by any improper ways.
I dislike death indeed, but there is that which I dislike more than death, and, therefore, there are occasions when I will not avoid danger.   —*Mencius*

The standard of conduct lies with one's own self; the testing of it lies with other men.
He who does not follow the Divine Path when standard and test are both clear may be likened to one who, when leaving a house, does not go by the door,

or, when traveling abroad, does not keep to the straight road.

To seek in this way, is it not a thing that is impossible?   —*Lieh Tzu*

Duke Wen of Chin put an army in the field with the intention of attacking the Duke of Wei. Where at Tzu Ch'u threw back his head and laughed aloud.

On being asked the reason for his behavior, he replied: "I was thinking about the experience of a neighbor of mine, who was escorting his wife on a visit to her own family. On the way, he came across a woman tending silk worms who attracted him greatly, and he fell into conversation with her. Happening to look up, what should he see but his own wife also receiving the attentions of an admirer! It was the recollection of this incident that made me laugh."

The Duke saw the point and immediately turned home with his army. And none too soon—before he returned an invading force had crossed his northern frontier.   —*Lieh Tzu*

Who is the wife of one cannot eat the rice of two.
                                                        —*Anonymous*

In the husband fidelity, in the wife obedience.
                                                        —*Anonymous*

Men may fear a slip of the tongue; women, a slip of their virtue.   —*Anonymous*

It is not the wine that makes the man drunk; man intoxicates himself. It is not beauty that beguiles a man; man beguiles himself.   —*Anonymous*

Because of the drinking of wine, passions are excited, and the wine demon changes and becomes the demon of fornication.   —*Anonymous*

A man is physically stronger than a woman, but

against an aggressive wife his hands are helpless.
—*Shu Shuehmou*

Teach your sons so that the straightforward may yet be mild, the gentle may yet be dignified, the strong not tyrannical, and the impetuous not arrogant.
—*Mencius*

When we have established our character by the practice of the filial course so as to make our name famous in future ages, and thereby glorify our parents—this is the end of filial piety.

It commences with the service of the parents; it proceeds to the service of the ruler; it is completed by the establishment of character.
—*The Hsiao King*

If a man does not walk in the right path, it will not be walked in even by his wife and children.

If he does not order men according to the right way, he will not be able to get the obedience of even his wife and children.
—*Mencius*

Those who have discharged their duty as children will in their turn have dutiful children of their own, while the obstinate and disrespectful produce offspring of the same character.

To convince you, only observe the rain from the thatched roof, where drop follows drop without the least variation.
—*Anonymous*

Just as the same tree may produce sweet and sour fruit, the same mother may birth both a virtuous and a vicious progeny.
—*Anonymous*

It is said that children suck their mothers when they are young, but is it not true that they do likewise with their fathers when they are grown up?
—*Anonymous*

One may give up a father though he be a magistrate, but not a mother though she be a beggar.
—*Anonymous*

It is virtuous manners which constitute the excellence of a neighborhood.

If a man in selecting a residence does not fix on one where such manners prevail, how can he be wise?

—*Confucius*

Men and women who know each other easily are cheap lovers; persons who easily make friends are not lifelong friends. —*Tut-Tut*

A great lover loves women, but one who loves women is not necessarily a great lover.

A beautiful woman often has a tragic life, but not all those who have tragic lives are beautiful.

—*Chang Chao*

The Master said: "Yew, shall I teach you what knowledge is? When you know a thing to hold that you know it, and when you do not know a thing to allow that you do not know it—this is knowledge."

—*Confucius*

A single conversation across the table with a wise man is better than ten years of mere study of books.

—*Anonymous*

He who teaches me for a day is my father for a lifetime. —*Anonymous*

Scholars are their country's treasure and the richest ornaments at a feast. —*Anonymous*

To feed a scholar and not love him is to treat him like a pig.

To love him and not respect him is to keep him like a domestic animal. —*Mencius*

A girl who flirts with her looks is not chaste; a scholar who flirts with his knowledge is not honest.

—*Tut-Tut*

One who can read the wordless book of life should

be able to write striking lines; one who understands the truth which is difficult to express by words is qualified to grasp the highest Zen wisdom.

—Chang Chao

He who from day to day recognizes what he does not yet have, and from month to month does not forget what he has attained to, may be said to love to learn.

—Confucius

Heaven's plan in the production of mankind is this: that they who are first informed should instruct those who are later in being informed, and they who first apprehend the principles should instruct those who are slower to do so.

—Mencius

They who know the truth are not equal to those who love it, and they who love it are not equal to those who find pleasure in it.

—Confucius

Great knowledge is wide and comprehensive; small knowledge is partial and restricted.

Great speech is exact and complete; small speech is merely so much talk.

—Chuang Tzu

Although a sword is sharp, without the frequent use of the grindstone, it will not cut.

Though a man's natural abilities be excellent, without learning he will not rise high.

The spirits may be good and the viands admirable, but until you taste them you do not know their flavor.

Principles may be good, but until you learn them you do not know their value.

Hence it is by learning that a man knows his deficiencies.

—Han Ying

The Master said, "Learning without thought is labor lost; thought without learning is perilous."

—Confucius

Government

King Wan looked on his people as he would on a man who was wounded, and he looked toward the right path as if he could not see it. —*Mencius*

The king is the strength of the weak in countries with royal sovereignty as crying is the strength of children. —*Anonymous*

The emperor is the father of his people, not a master to be served by slaves. —*Anonymous*

A sage teaches without changing the people, and a wise man obtains good government without altering the laws. —*Kan Lung*

To govern means to *rectify*. If you lead on the people with correctness, who will not dare to be correct. —*Confucius*

Guide the people with government measures and control or regulate them by the threat of punishment, and the people will try to keep out of jail but will have no sense of honor or shame.
Guide the people by virtue and control and regulate them by respect, and the people will have a sense of honor and respect. —*Confucius*

Only the benevolent ought to be in high stations. When a man destitute of benevolence is in a high station, he thereby disseminates his wickedness among all below him. —*Mencius*

If the one in authority is not enlightened, one can

know that those beneath him are in the dark.

—*Anonymous*

Virtue alone is not sufficient for the exercise of government; laws alone cannot carry themselves into practice. —*Mencius*

Kindness is greater than law. —*Anonymous*

A severe law-enforcement officer produces thieves.

—*Anonymous*

The greater the number of laws and enactments, the more thieves and robbers there will be. —*Lao Tzu*

In enacting laws, rigor is indispensable; in executing them, mercy. —*Anonymous*

Break the regulations, rather than kill an innocent man. —*Tsochuan*

The character of the ruler is like wind, and the character of the common people is like grass . . . it is the grass that bends in the direction of the wind. —*Confucius*

Honor the worthy and maintain the talented to give distinction to the virtuous. —*Mencius*

Without the wisdom of the learned, the clown could not be governed; without the labor of the clown, the learned could not be fed. —*Anonymous*

To show compassion toward the people by remitting the severity of the taxes is the virtue of the prince; and to offer up their possessions, putting aside their private differences, is the duty of the people.

—*Anonymous*

Respect shown by inferiors to superiors is called giving the noble the observance due to rank.
Respect shown by superiors is called giving honor to

群后亮功圖

帝舜　四岳　臯陶　契　伯夷　龍　伯禹　后稷　伯益　后夔　垂

十二州牧

talent and virtue; the rightness in each case is the same. —*Mencius*

As the restrictions and prohibitions are multiplied in a country, the people grow poorer and poorer. When the people are subjected to overmuch government, confusion reigns across the land. When the people are skilled in many cunning arts, strange are the objects of luxury that appear. —*Lao Tzu*

Against open crimes, punishments can create a barrier; but secret offenses are difficult for the law to reach. —*Anonymous*

If we make for men pecks and bushels to measure their wares, even by means of those pecks and bushels we would be teaching them to steal.
If we make for them tallies and seals to secure their good faith, even by means of those tallies and seals we shall be teaching them to steal. —*Chuang Tzu*

It is equally criminal in the governor, and in the governed, to violate the laws. —*Anonymous*

Killing a bad monarch is not murder. —*Mencius*

In the highest antiquity, the people did not know that they had rulers. In the next age, they loved and praised them. In the next, they feared them. In the next, they despised them. —*Lao Tzu*

When a country is well-governed, poverty and a mean condition are things to be ashamed of.
When a country is ill-governed, riches and honor are things to be ashamed of. —*Confucius*

A country that knows how to produce strength but not how to control it may be said to be a country that attacks itself. —*Lord Shang*

Let the official who has time to spare devote it to

study; let the student who has time to spare devote it to public affairs. —*Tzu Hsia*

A country where uniformity of purpose has been established for one year will be strong for ten years; where uniformity of purpose has been established for ten years, it will be strong for a hundred years; where uniformity of purpose has been established for a hundred years, it will be strong for a thousand years. —*Lord Shang*

If a country is rich but administered as if it were poor, then it is said to be doubly rich, and the doubly rich are strong.

If the country is poor but administered as if it were rich, it is said to be doubly poor, and the doubly poor are weak. —*Lord Shang*

If a man should wish to gain a kingdom for himself, and to effect this by what he does, he will not succeed. The kingdom is a spirit-like thing and cannot be achieved by active doing.

He who would so win it destroys it.

He who would hold it in his grasp loses it. —*Lao Tzu*

The commander of the forces of a large state may be carried off, but the will of even a common man cannot be taken from him. —*Confucius*

Would you know politics? Read history! —*Anonymous*

Combat

When people are stupid, they think force easy but cleverness difficult; but if the world is clever, then it thinks knowledge easy but force difficult. —*Lord Shang*

No man will confide in one who shows himself as aggressive. And he whom no man confides in will remain solitary and without support. —*Lieh Tzu*

He who strikes with a sharp point will not himself be safe for long. —*Lao Tzu*

A moment's forbearance will preserve your person. —*Inscription on a sword*

The superior man moves his lips, the common man moves his fists. —*Anonymous*

When one by force subdues men, they do not submit to him in their heart. They submit because their strength is not adequate to resist. When one subdues men by virtue in their heart's core, they are pleased and submit sincerely, as was the case with the seventy disciples in their submission to Confucius. —*Mencius*

Weapons, however beautiful, are instruments of evil omen, hateful, it may be said, to all creatures. These sharp instruments are not the tools of the superior man—he uses them solely on the compulsion of necessity. Calm and repose are his true weapons, while victory by force of arms a painful resort. To consider weapons desirable would be to delight in the slaughter of men; and he who delights in the slaughter of men cannot get his true will on earth. He who has killed multitudes of men should weep for them with the bitterest of grief. —*Lao Tzu*

A good fighter flees from the moment's danger. —*Anonymous*

A skillful warrior strikes a decisive blow and stops. He does not continue his attack to assert his mastery. He will strike the blow, but be on his guard against being vain or arrogant over his success. He strikes it as

四征弗庭圖

a matter of necessity, but not from a wish of mastery. —*Lao Tzu*

Never beat a man on a wound nor curse him about a disgrace. —*Anonymous*

Hear the pig's cries at the butchers at midnight, and you know what the battlefield is like. —*Anonymous*

The wise soldier knows how to marshal the ranks where there are no ranks, can bare the arms to fight where there are no arms to bare, advances against the enemy where there is no enemy. Thus it is that when opposing weapons are crossed, he who deplores the situation conquers. —*Lao Tzu*

In war, think always of how to save lives. —*Chen Chiju*

Gentleness brings victory to him who attacks and safety to him who defends. Those whom Heaven would save, it fences around with gentleness. —*Lao Tzu*

He who advances may fight, but he who retreats may take care of himself. —*Anonymous*

A military man who does not talk lightly of war is also a cultured man; a cultured man who does not rest with his smug opinions has something of the conqueror's spirit. —*Chang Chao*

Medicine is for saving life but in the hands of quacks can kill people. Soldiers are for killing people, but in the hands of wise rulers can save people's lives. —*Chen Chiju*

Military schemes to be of use must be in the heart, not in books. —*Yoh Fei*

Men who work on the waters do not shrink from

meeting sharks and whales—that is the courage of the fisherman. Men who work on the land and do not shrink from meeting tigers and rhinoceroses—that is the courage of the hunter. When men see sharp weapons crossed before them and look on death as going home—that is the courage of the determined soldier. —Chuang Tzu

To learn kung fu fully one must embody the entire kung fu philosophy. Without the mind the body is useless. —Yew Ching Wong

The mind (i) commands, strength (li) goes along, and internal energy (chi) follows. —Anonymous.

When an old man is able to defeat many attackers, how could it be due to his strength? —Wang Chung-yueh

Permeate the body with chi so that it may be pliable and thus follow the direction of the mind. —Wu Yu-seong

Strength by itself is not equal to knowledge, and knowledge is not equal to training; but combine knowledge with training, and one will get strength. —Anonymous

A hoodlum doesn't have the patience to become proficient at kung fu. He prefers to buy a weapon, not develop one. —Anonymous

They are not good fists that fight, nor good words that curse. —Anonymous

The true hero hardens his nature and controls his mind; the mock variety makes a show of his talents and flies off his temper. —Tut-Tut

Others know him not, only he alone knows others. A hero is without match because he is the master of this principle. —Wang Chung-yueh

When facing an adversary . . . manifest suddenly and conceal suddenly.   —*Wang Chung-yueh*

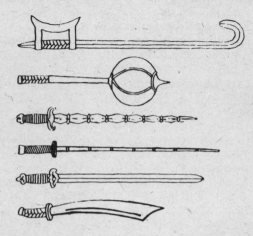

There should never be more than three blows thrown in a violent encounter. An opponent is permitted to strike once, sometimes twice, but the third blow is always thrown by the kung fu man.

—*Anonymous*

Boxing is like taking a walk; striking an enemy is like snapping your fingers.   —*Anonymous*

Correct hitting is invisible. An enemy should fall without seeing your hands.
—*Popular proverb of Shansi kung fu men*

There are other techniques of self-defense; disregarding their differences they are similar in that the strong is able to overcome the weak, and the fast is able to prevail over the slow. The wise man knows that there are natural abilities that require no study.
—*Wang Chung-yueh*

On looking upward he appears too high to be accessible and on looking downward he seems unfathomable. On his advance, the distance should seem lengthened and on his retreat, his advance should appear rapid.   —Wang Chung-yueh

A brave soldier is not violent.
A skillful fighter does not lose his temper.
A great general wins without a battle.
A mighty ruler governs through humility.
This is known as the Virtue of Not Striving.

—Lao Tzu

The aim of tai chi is to sacrifice oneself to comply with an adversary. Yet many regard this as a mistake similar to abandoning the near to seek the far. This attitude could be correctly likened to making a mistake of a fraction of an inch and end up missing the target by a thousand miles. Therefore, in the study of the art, the wise student uses his discretion.

—Wang Chung-yueh

True kung fu is rooted in the feet. It develops in the legs, is directed by the waist, and functions through the fingers.   —Chang San-feng

A strength of one thousand pounds can be repulsed with four ounces.   —Anonymous

Store force like one drawing a bow; issue force like shooting an arrow.

—Wu Yu-seong

The characteristic of the long fist is comparable to a long river; its waters run continuously and endlessly.   —Wu Yu-seong

The form [of tai chi] should be likened to that of an eagle preying on the hunted rabbit and the attitude like that of the cat when about to pounce on the mouse.   —Wu Yu-seong

A phony kung fu man shoots out of his hand ferociously, but his punch contains no true strength. A

master is not so flamboyant, but his touch is as heavy as a mountain.
—*Chueh Yuan*

Beginning students block an assault, experienced kung fu men attack after blocking, but true masters no longer have the need to block.
—*Anonymous*

A small injustice can be drowned by a cup of wine; a great injustice can be drowned only by the sword.
—*Chang Chao*

The superior man takes three years to revenge an enemy; the common man has his revenge at once.
—*Anonymous*

Human Nature

In painting the tiger, you may delineate his skin but not his bones; in your acquaintance with a man, you may know his face but not his heart.
—*Anonymous*

The fishes, though deep in the water, may be hooked; the birds, though high in the air, may be shot; but man's secret thoughts are out of our reach.
The heavens may be measured; the earth may be surveyed; the heart of man only is not to be known.
—*Anonymous*

A man who has a beautiful soul always has some beautiful things to say, but a man who says beautiful things does not necessarily have a beautiful soul.
—*Confucius*

A true man will always be found to have courage,

but a courageous man will not always be found to have true manhood. —Confucius

The virtuous will be sure to speak correctly, but those whose speech is good may not always be virtuous.

Men of principle are sure to be bold, but those who are bold may not always be men of principle. —Confucius

The man of first-rate excellence is virtuous independently of instruction; he of the middling class gains virtue after instruction, but the lowest order of men are vicious and self-centered in spite of instruction. —Anonymous

The man of worth is really great without being proud; the common man is proud without being really great. —Anonymous

Humility is a good thing, but overhumility is near to crookedness; silence is a virtue, but undue silence bespeaks a deceitful mind. —Tut-Tut

The braggart is seldom loyal, the glib talker seldom honest. —Tut-Tut

He who promises lightly is sure to keep but little faith; he who is continually thinking things easy is sure to find them difficult. —Lao Tzu

The sincerity of him who assents to everything must be small, and he who praises you inordinately to your face must be altogether false. —Anonymous

Who does evil and is afraid of letting it be known has still a seed of good in his evil; who does good and is anxious to have it known has still a root of evil in his good. —Tut-Tut

Probably there are none in the world who at first do evil without reluctance; but when they have repeated it once or twice the mind becomes daring; hands and feet become habituated, and the conscience is by degrees annihilated.

·—*The Sacred Edict, Explanation of the Laws*

The gentleman fears God's will, fears the great man, fears the words of the sages. The rascal fears nothing.

—*Mencius*

There was once a man of the Ch'i State who had a burning lust for gold. Rising early one morning, he dressed and went down to the marketplace, where he proceeded to seize and carry off the gold from a money-changer's shop. He was arrested by the police who were puzzled to know why he committed the theft when everybody was about.

"When I was taking the gold," he replied, "I did not see anybody at all; what I saw was the gold, and nothing but the gold." —*Lieh Tzu*

The avarice of man is like a snake trying to swallow an elephant. —*Anonymous*

Of those men whose talent is inconsiderable while their station is eminent, and of those whose knowledge is small while their schemes are large—there are few who do not become miserable. —*Ye-King*

He was a man who had a little ability but had not learned the doctrines of the superior man.

He was just qualified to bring death upon himself, but for nothing more. —*Mencius*

Who is narrow of vision cannot be bighearted; who is narrow of spirit cannot take long, easy strides.

—*Tut-Tut*

He who stops short where stopping short is not allowable will stop short in everything.

He who behaves shabbily to those whom he ought to treat well will behave shabbily to all. —*Mencius*

Those who excel in beauty become vain; those who excel in strength become violent. To such, it is useless to speak of Divine Knowledge.

—*Lieh Tzu*

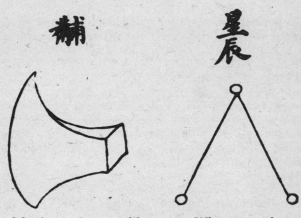

Men's passions are like water. When water has once flowed over, it cannot be easily restored; when the passions have once been indulged, they cannot easily be restrained.

Water must be kept in dikes; the passions must be regulated by the laws of propriety.   —*Anonymous*

A man is ignorant of his own failings just as the ox is unconscious of its great strength.   —*Anonymous*

Though the life of a man be short of a hundred years, he gives himself as much anxiety as if he were to live to a thousand.   —*Anonymous*

A man having lost his ax suspected his neighbor's son of having taken it. Certain peculiarities in his gait, his countenance, and his speech marked him as a thief. In his actions, his movements, and in fact his whole demeanor it was plainly written that he and no other had stolen the ax.

By and by, however, while digging in a dell, the owner came across the missing implement. The next day when he saw his neighbor's son again, he could find no trace of the guilt in his speech, actions, or movements that he saw the day before. —*Lieh Tzu*

The disease of men is this—that they neglect their own fields and go weed the fields of others.

Thus it may be said that what they require from others is great, while what they lay upon themselves is light. —*Mencius*

It is the way of Heaven to take from those who have too much and give to those who have too little. But the way of man is not so. He takes away from those who have to little, to add to his own superabundance. —*Lao Tzu*

The archer, contending for a piece of earthenware puts forth all his skill. If the prize be a buckle of brass, he shoot timorously; if it be for an article of gold, he shoots as if he were blind. —*Chuang Tzu*

The ignorant man is a hasty man.

He sees the egg and immediately begins to look for the cock that is to be hatched from it.

He sees the bow and immediately looks for the roast dove brought down by its arrows. —*Ch'ang Wu Tzu*

In ancient times men learned with a view to their own improvement.

Nowadays men learn with a view toward the approval of others. —*Confucius*

He who is a good judge of men corrects what he hears by what he sees; he who is not a good judge of men corrupts what he sees by what he hears. —*Tut-Tut*

The evil of men is that they like to be teachers of others. —*Mencius*

The man who is fond of daring and is dissatisfied with poverty will proceed to insubordination, as will the man who is not virtuous when you carry your dislike of him to an extreme. —*Confucius*

When an inferior man plans to injure a gentleman, his heart is cruel, his plans are well layed out, and his actions are firm; therefore the gentleman can seldom escape.

When a gentleman intends to punish a lower person, his heart is kind, his plans are incomplete, and he cannot quite go the limit; therefore more often than not he himself is victimized by it. —*Tut-Tut*

Only the highest and lowest characters don't change. —*Confucius*

When a man at forty is the object of dislike, he will always continue what he is. —*Confucius*

In youth not humble as befits a junior; in manhood doing nothing worthy to be handed down; and living to an old age—this is to be a pest. —*Confucius*

Ardent and yet not upright, stupid and yet not attentive, simple and yet not sincere—such persons I do not understand. —*Confucius*

I have lived fifty years to know the mistakes of forty-nine. —*Chupoyo*

When a bird is about to die, its notes are mournful. When a man is about to die, his words are good. —*Confucius*

As the scream of an eagle is heard when it passes overhead, so a man's name remains after death. —*Anonymous*

The way of the people is this—if they have a certain livelihood they will have a fixed heart.

If they have not a certain livelihood they have not a fixed heart.

And if they have not a fixed heart there is nothing which they will not do in the way of self-abandonment, of moral deflection, of depravity, and of wild license. —*Mencius*

Rich men look forward to the years that are to come, but the poor man has to think only of what is immediately before him. —*Anonymous*

Those who despise money end up sponging on their friends. —*Chang Chao*

The common man has strong natural prejudices where he feels love and affection, prejudices where he despises and dislikes; prejudices where he stands in awe and reverence, prejudices where he feels sorrow and compassion, prejudices where he is arrogant and rude.

Thus it is that there are few men in the world who love and at the same time know the bad qualities of the object of their love, or who hate and yet know the excellencies of the object of their hatred. —*The Great Learning*

He who is cold examines not the quality of the cloth; he who is hungry tarries not for choice of meats.

When cold and hunger come upon men, honesty and shame depart. —*Ch'ao Ts'o*

By nature, men are born nearly alike; by practice they get to be far apart. —*Confucius*

Where views and dispositions agree, the most distant will unite in friendship; where they disagree, even relations will soon be at emnity. —*Anonymous*

Sarcasm is the last refuge of the defeated wit. —*Anonymous*

In the present world which is run by sophisticated city folks, only children and simpletons speak the truth.
—*Anonymous*

What the world reverences may not be treated with respect.
—*Lao Tzu*

A police officer may catch thieves with one hand and receive booty with the other. A man may join in condemning adultery but love to take a peep at the adulteress.
—*Shu Shuehmou*

A poor man, though living in a crowded mart, will go unnoticed.
A rich man, though dwelling on a remote mountain, will be visited by his distant relatives.
—*Foo Chow*

The ancients praised those who were proud though poor and not snobbish though rich.
Now in modern days it is difficult to find the poor who are not snobbish and the rich who are not haughty.
—*Chang Chao*

You can see the man in the child, just as you can see the horse in its hoofs.
—*Anonymous*

Rotton wood cannot be carved.
—*Anonymous*

The great hypocrite weeps to make people believe him; women and cowards weep to make people pity them.
—*Tut-Tut*

A literary man discussing wars and battles is mostly an armchair strategist; a military man who discusses literature relies mostly on rumors picked up from hearsay.
—*Chang Chao*

The clever man often worries; the loyal person is often overworked.
—*Tut-Tut*

It is difficult to be muddle-headed and difficult to be intelligent.

It is even more difficult to graduate from intelligence into muddle-headedness. —*Cheng Panchiao*

Man's nature to good is like the tendency of water to flow downward.
There are none but have not this tendency to good just as all water flows downward. —*Mencius*

A gem is not polished without rubbing nor a man perfected without trials.
—*Inscription on the temple of Everlasting Harmony*

The wise are free from perplexities, the virtuous from anxiety, and the bold from fear. —*Anonymous*

The benevolent man loves others; the intelligent man understands others. —*Anonymous*

Men who are possessed of intelligent virtue and prudence in affairs will generally be found to have suffered sickness and troubles. —*Mencius*

To desire to be honored is the common mind of men, and all men have in themselves that which is truly honorable.
Only they do not think of it. —*Mencius*

He who knows his stupidity is not very stupid. He who knows that he is under a delusion is not greatly deluded. He who is greatly deluded will never shake off his delusion; he who is very stupid will all his life not become intelligent. —*Chuang Tzu*

Material possessions and wealth are like the soot that collects under the boiler. When it is differently distributed, the life is spoken of as different. But to say that life is different in different lives and better in one than another is the wisdom of the fools. —*Chuang Tzu*

Though a thousand miles apart, a thread will draw together those who are decreed for each other.
—*Anonymous*

When a good mirror meets an ugly owner, a good inkstone meets a vulgar person, and a good sword finds itself in the hands of a common general, there is nothing these things can do about it.   —*Chang Chao*

The slow horse is destined to receive the whip; the worthless man will finally receive punishment.
—*Anonymous*

Though brothers are very near relations, the differences of fortune widely separate them.   —*Anonymous*

It is not Heaven that does not deal impartially with men, but men who bring ruin upon themselves.
—*Shoo King*

Human relationship may injure you, but fate does not.   —*Anonymous*

A physician may cure disease, but he cannot heal fate.   —*Anonymous*

Death cannot make rich one whom fate has made poor.   —*Anonymous*

The fortunate eat food; the unfortunate eat bitterness.   —*Anonymous*

When one's fortunate time comes, he meets a good friend; when one has lost his luck, he meets a beautiful woman.   —*Anonymous*

When a man obtains a large sum without having earned it, if it does not make him very happy, it will certainly make him very unhappy.   —*Anonymous*

A horse may have the strength to run a thousand miles, but without a rider it knows not where to go; a man may have the ambition to scale the clouds, but without luck he cannot go on.   —*Anonymous*

What exists in the morning, we cannot be certain of in the evening; what exists in the evening, we cannot calculate upon in the morning.

The fortunes of men are as variable as the winds and the clouds of Heaven. —*Anonymous*

Prosperity in business is not a sign or proof of the rectitude of one's principles.

That the wicked have plenty to eat is no indication of the approval of Heaven. —*Foo Chow*

If you wish to eat the food of an official, you must be born with the teeth of an official. —*Anonymous*

A foolish man always has a good horse to ride; a clever woman usually gets a stupid husband as a partner.

—*Anonymous*

Happiness is lighter than a feather, but no one knows how to support it; calamity is heavier than the earth and yet no one knows how to avoid it.

—*Khieh-yu, the madman of Khu*

Ke Loo asked about serving the spirits of the dead. The Master said, "While you are not able to serve men, how can you serve their spirits?"

Ke Loo added, "I venture to ask about death."

He was answered, "While you do not know about life, how can you know about death?" —*Confucius*

Everybody dies. How he dies is important.

Sometimes a death has the weight of the Tai Shan Mountain; sometimes it is lighter than a feather. —*Szema Chien*

There once was a man, Tung-men Wu of Wei, who when his son died testified no grief.

His house steward said to him: "The love you bore your son could hardly equal that of any other parent. Why, then, do you not mourn for him now that he is dead?"

"There was a time," replied Tung-men Wu, "when I had no son. During the whole period that elapsed before my son was born, I never had occasion to grieve. Now that my son is dead, I am only in the same condition as I was before I had a son. What reason have I, then, to mourn?"
—*Lieh Tzu*

Though a tree is a thousand *chang* in height, its leaves must fall down and return to the root.
—*Anonymous*

How do we not know that love of life is not an illusion and that the dislike of death is not a young person's losing his way and not knowing that he is really going home?

Li Ki was a daughter of the border warden of Ai. When the ruler of a neighboring state first got possession of her, she wept till tears wetted the front of her dress. But when she came to the place of the king, shared with him his luxurious coach, ate at his table, then she regretted that she had wept.

How do we know that the dead do not repent of their former craving for life.
—*Chuang Tzu*

An excellent thing was death in the eyes of the ancients.

It gives rest to the good and subdues the wicked.

Death is the boundary line of virtue.
—*Lieh Tzu*

Men feel the joy of life, but they do not realize its bitterness.

They feel the weariness of old age, but not its peacefulness.

They think of the evils of death, but not of the repose which it confers.
—*Lieh Tzu*

Man eats of the Earth for a lifetime; the Earth eats man in a single mouthful.
—*Anonymous*

The Yellow Emperor said: "If my spirit returns through the gates whence it came, and my bones go

back to the source from which they sprang, where does the Ego continue to exist?"
—*Lieh Tzu*

The ancients described death as the loosening of the cord on which God has suspended the life. When we look on a dead body all we can point to are the fagots that have been consumed; but the fire is transmitted elsewhere, and we know not that it is over and ended.
—*Chuang Tzu*

Can the swallow know the wild goose's course?
—*Anonymous*

Plants surpass men in recognizing spring.
—*Anonymous*

The birth of a man is at the same time the birth of his sorrow.
—*Chuang Tzu*

Not even the cleverest doctor can save himself.
—*Anonymous*

It is easier to stand pain than to stand an itch; the bitter taste is easier to bear than the sour. —*Chang Chao*

Practical Advice

Think twice . . . and then say nothing. —*Anonymous*

When there is a feast of mere words there is bound to be a famine of intelligence.
—*Anonymous*

Alas . . . . Four horses cannot overtake the tongue.
—*Confucius*

If you wish to know what most engages a man's thoughts, you have only to listen to his conversation. —Anonymous

He who keeps his mouth open and spends his breath in the continual promotion of his affairs will never, in all his life, experience safety. —Lao Tzu

Disaster comes out of the mouth, not into it. —Anonymous

Do not open your heart to the grim silent one; guard your tongue before the garrulous fool. —Tut-Tut

He who speaks without modesty will find it difficult to make his words good. —Anonymous

If a person asks something that is evil, do not tell him; if he wants to tell something evil, do not ask; if he speaks about evil, do not listen; if he wishes to quarrel, do not have discourse with him. —Hsun Tze

Preserving harmony between men rests solely on the word *forbearance*, or, as it may be called, the art of eating down an injury. —The Sacred Edict

Talk not of your personal success to one who has failed; forget not your failures in your moment of success. —Tut-Tut

Better feed people than bait them with words. —Shu Shuehmou

Praise a man at his back and not his face, and he will really appreciate it when he hears about it. —Shu Shuehmou

If one has to praise someone, rather do it by word of mouth than by pen; if there are persons that must be castigated, also do it by word of mouth rather than by writing. —Chang Chao

Fear not when men speak evil of you; fear lest you should do evil.
—*Anonymous*

A person who likes to drop names can fool the innocent, but not the people with a better background.
—*Shu Shuehmou*

In speaking to the ruler of a country, one must look out for three things:
To talk before you are asked is called "impulsiveness." To fail to talk when you are asked is called "lack of candor." And to talk without noticing the ruler's mood is called "blindness."
—*Confucius*

True words are not fine; fine words are not always true.
—*Lao Tzu*

Do not speak lightly; your words are your own.
Do not say, this is of little importance, or that no one can hold my tongue for me; words are not to be cast away.
Every word finds its answer; every good deed has its recompense.
—*She King*

Prudence will carry a man all over the world, but the impetuous will find every step difficult. —*Anonymous*

He who requires much from himself and little from others will keep himself from being the object of resentment.
—*Confucius*

Falling hurts least those who fly low. —*Anonymous*

Forgive your servants (or friends) when they offend you.
Do not forgive them when they offend others.
—*Chen Chiju*

Do not anxiously hope for what has not yet come.
Do not vainly regret that which is already past.
—*Anonymous*

If a man takes no thought of what is distant he will find sorrow near at hand. —*Confucius*

It is better to owe the world a debt than to have the world owe you a debt. —*Tsao Tsao*

To correct an evil that already exists is not so good as to foresee and prevent it. —*Anonymous*

In the midst of great joy do not promise to give a man anything.
In the midst of great anger do not answer a man's letter. —*Anonymous*

He who can suppress a moment's anger may prevent many days' sorrow. —*Anonymous*

When your horse is on the brink of the precipice it is too late to pull in the rein; when calamity is upon you repentance is too late. —*Anonymous*

Seek not every quality in one individual. —*Shoo King*

Do not forget little kindnesses, and do not remember small faults. —*Anonymous*

Do unto others as you would have others do unto you.
But better not expect others to do unto you what you would do unto them. —*Chen Chiju*

Who is indignant at false gossip invites rumor; who is pleased with words of praise attracts the flatterers. —*Tut-Tut*

The evidence of others is not comparable to personal experience; not is "I heard" as good as "I saw." —*Anonymous*

Do not love idleness and hate labor; do not be diligent in the beginning and in the end, lazy.
—*Anonymous*

Whenever you do a thing, act so that it will give your friends no occasion for regret and your foes no cause for joy.
—*Tut-Tut*

Without a clear mirror a woman cannot know the state of her own face; without a true friend a man cannot discern the errors of his own actions.
—*Anonymous*

Though powerful medicines be nauseous to the taste, they are good for the disease; though candid advice be unpleasant to the ear, it is profitable for one's conduct.
—*Anonymous*

Drink by all means, but do not make drunken scenes; have women by all means, but do not destroy your health; work for money by all means, but do not let it blot out your conscience; get mad about something, but do not go beyond reason.
—*Chang Chao*

When you find a person worthy to talk and fail to talk to him, you have missed your man.
When you find a man unworthy to talk to and you talk to him you have missed [i.e., wasted] your words.

A wise man neither misses his man nor misses his words.
—*Confucius*

When walking with two men, let each one serve you as your teacher.
Pick out the good points in one, and imitate them; and the bad points in the other and try to correct them in yourself.
—*Anonymous*

You can deceive your superiors but not your inferiors.
—*Anonymous*

What a man dislikes in his superiors let him not display in the treatment of his inferiors. What he dislikes in inferiors let him not display in the service of his superiors.
—*The Great Learning*

Do not open the doors for favorites for whom you will receive contempt.
Do not be ashamed of mistakes and thus make them crimes.
—*Shoo King*

When duty knocks at your door open it wide.
Ignore it, and you will have many unwelcome duties.
—*Anonymous*

The partial becomes complete; the crooked, straight; the empty, full; the worn out, new.
He whose desires are few gets them; he whose desires are many goes astray.
—*Lao Tzu*

Be a day lily among grass.
Do not be a cuckoo among the birds.   —*Chang Chao*

He who advances with precipitation will retire with speed.
—*Mencius*

Better to go than to send.   —*Anonymous*

Follow what is right and you will be fortunate.
Do not follow what is right and you will be unfortunate.

The results are only shadows and echoes of our actions.
  —*Counsels of the Great Yu, 2255* B.C.

Deviate an inch, lose a thousand miles.
  —*Anonymous*

So live that your life may be a poem. Arrange things so that they look like they are in a painting.
  —*Chang Chao*

Those who respect themselves will be held honorable, but he who thinks lightly of himself will be held cheap by the world. —*Anonymous*

A single skill enables one to make a living; too many abilities make one a slave. —*Tut-Tut*

If one works only for what he is paid, sometimes in life he will find he will not be worthy of what he wants to work for. —*Anonymous*

If the body be toiled and does not rest, it becomes worn out; if the spirit be used without cessation, it becomes toiled, and when toiled . . . exhausted.
  —*Chuang Tzu*

A bright future often depends on clearing up a shady past. —*Anonymous*

Remind a gentleman of shame and threaten a sneak with pain. It always works. —*Chang Chao*

A man should say, I am not concerned that I have no place, I am concerned how I may fit myself for one. I am not concerned that I am not known, I seek to be worthy to be known. —*Confucius*

If a man's house is not secluded, his mind does not wander far; if a man's face does not show a little sadness, his thoughts are not deep. —*Tut-Tut*

Questions of right and wrong (with references to

men's characters) are every day arising: if not listened to, they die away of themselves. —*Anonymous*

A man's prosperous or declining condition may be gathered from the proportion of his waking to sleeping hours. —*Anonymous*

If a man's wishes be few, his health will be flourishing; if he has many anxious thoughts, his constitution will decay. —*Anonymous*

A man's countenance is a sufficient index of his prosperity or adversity, without anyone's asking him any questions. —*Anonymous*

Mark those who manage their affairs well . . . also mark those who do not do so. —*Shoo King*

By looking at a man's faults, you know the man's character. —*Confucius*

Of all the parts of a man's body there is none more excellent than the pupil of the eye. The pupil cannot be used to hide a man's wickedness.

If within the breast all be correct, the pupil is bright. If within the breast all be not correct, the pupil is dull. Listen to a man's words and look at the pupil of his eye. How can a man conceal his character? —*Mencius*

By a long journey we know a horse's strength: so the length of days reveals a man's heart. —*Anonymous*

Where there is musk there will, of course, be perfume; it will not be necessary to stand in the wind. Talent and worth will manifest themselves without resorting to trickery. —*Foo Chow*

On occasions of a great or difficult crisis, you see a man's stature; on occasions of good luck or mishap, you see a man's great or small mind; in moments of satisfaction or anger, you see a man's degree of moral culture; in a man's refusal or acceptance of a course of action with or against the crowd, you see a man's sense of judgement. —*Tut-Tut*

Would you know the character of a ruler prince, examine his ministers; would you understand the disposition of any man, look at his companions; would you know that of a father, observe his son.
—*Anonymous*

In judging people, judge a common man by where he stands in important matters, but judge a great man by watching what he does in little things. —*Chen Chiju*

If what we see is doubtful, how can we believe what is spoken behind the back?
—*Inscription in the "Celestial Influence Temple"*

It is easy to convince a wise man, but to reason with a fool is a difficult undertaking. —*Anonymous*

He who has not faith in others shall find no faith in them. —*Lao Tzu*

Keep your mind busy to accomplish things; keep your mind open to understand things. —*Tut-Tut*

Racing and hunting excite man's heart to madness. —*Lao Tzu*

Today well lived makes every yesterday a dream of happiness, and every tomorrow a vision of hope. —*Anonymous*

Past events are as clear as a mirror; the future, as obscure as varnish. —*Anonymous*

A man may be considered to have a real desire for improvement if he daily recognized his deficiencies and at the end of the month does not forget what he has learned. —*Tzu Hsia*

The cautious seldom err. —*Confucius*

The tree that brushes the heavens grew from the tiniest sprout.
The most elegant pagoda, nine stories high, rose from a small pile of earth.
The journey of a thousand miles began with but a single step. —*Lao Tzu*

To go a little too far is as bad as not going far enough. —*Confucius*

He who wishes to know the road through the mountains must ask those who have already trodden it. —*Anonymous*

If a man does not receive guests at home, he will meet with very few hosts while abroad. —*Anonymous*

An old man has crossed more bridges than a young man has crossed streets. —*Anonymous*

Only those who take leisurely what the people of the world are busy about can be busy about what the people of the world take leisurely. —*Chang Chao*

Even in trifling pursuits there is sure to be something that is worthy of attention; yet, there is always the danger of the trifles becoming all-absorbing if carried too far. That is why the wise man does not engage in them. —*Tzu Hsia*

To have peace of mind not quite perfect is to deepen the awareness of peace; to enjoy pleasure not quite to the limit is to prolong the flavor of those pleasures. —*Tut-Tut*

Money sometimes prevents trouble; too much money breeds it. —*Tut-Tut*

Medicine cannot cure a false disease; wine cannot dispel real sorrow.
—*Anonymous*

Procrastination is the thief of time. —*Anonymous*

The cure of ignorance is study, as meat is that of hunger.
—*Anonymous*

Read a few more books and talk a little less.
—*Chen Chiju*

The difficulty is not in reading books, but in applying the truths to life, and the greatest difficulty is in remembering them. —*Chang Chao*

In making a candle we seek for light; in reading a book we seek for reason: light to illuminate a dark chamber, reason to enlighten a man's heart.
—*Anonymous*

The pen conveys one's meaning a thousand miles.
—*Anonymous*

It is more profitable to reread some old books than to read new ones, just as it is better to repair and add to an old temple than to build an entirely new one. —*Chang Chao*

The benefit of reading varies directly with one's experience in life. It is like looking at the moon.
A young reader may be compared to one seeing the moon through a single crack, a middle-aged reader seems to see it from an enclosed courtyard, and an old man seems to see it from an open terrace, with a complete view of the entire field. —*Chang Chao*

Give no indulgence to the wily and obsequious in order to make the unconscientious careful. —*She King*

The spontaneous gifts of Heaven are of high value; but the strength of perserverance gains the prize.
—*Anonymous*

If you would contract, you must first expand.
If you would weaken, you must first strengthen.
If you would tear down, you must first raise up.
If you would take, you must first give.
This is called the dawn of intelligence.   —Lao Tzu

To be fond of learning is to be near to cosmic knowledge.   —Doctrine of the Mean

The attempt, with what is not even, to produce what is even will only produce an uneven result.

The attempt, with what is certain, to make the uncertain certain will leave the uncertainty as it was.

He who uses only the sight of his eyes is acted on by what he sees; it is the intuition of the spirit that gives the assurance of certainty.

That the sight of the eyes is not equal to the intuition of the spirit is a thing long acknowledged. And yet stupid people rely on what they see—is it not sad?   —Chuang Tzu

He who has never tasted the bitterness of life has never known the sweetness of it all.   —Anonymous

A scholar's inkstone should be exquisite, but so should a businessman's. A concubine for pleasure should be beautiful, but so should also a concubine for continuing the family line.   —Chang Chao

When a wife feels unhappy and the husband shares her unhappiness, her unhappiness will vanish. But when a wife gets into a rage, it won't do for the husband to get into a rage.   —Shu Shuehmou

It is better to have an understanding wife than a pretty concubine, as it is better to have peace of mind than wealth.   —Chang Chao

If you love your son, be liberal in your punishments; if you hate your son, accustom him to luxuries.   —Chang Chao

A mother-in-law's smiles are like the April sun, unpredictable.
—*Anonymous*

All the universe is an inn; search not specially for a retreat of peace: all the people are your relatives; expect therefore troubles from them.
—*Tut-Tut*

If there be want of concord among members of the same family, other men will take advantage of it to injure them.
—*Anonymous*

The three great misfortunes in life are: in youth, to bury one's father; at middle age, to lose one's wife; and being old, to have no sons or daughters. —*Anonymous*

When we meet with difficulties we think of our relatives; but on the brink of danger we rely on our friends.
—*Anonymous*

It is not easy to stop the fire when water is at a distance; friends at hand are better than relations far off.
—*Anonymous*

Friends are not made, but discovered. —*Anonymous*

Friendship should be maintained without any presumption on the ground of one's superior age or station or the circumstances of his relatives.
Friendship with a man is friendship with his virtue and does not admit assumptions of superiority.
—*Mencius*

In serving a prince frequent remonstrances lead to disgrace; between friends, frequent reproofs make the friendship distant.
—*Confucius*

In friendship, honoring and respecting are what exist before any offers of gifts.
—*Mencius*

To meet with an old friend in a distant country may be compared to the delightfulness of rain after a long drought.
—*Anonymous*

The good-looking woman needs no paint.
—*Anonymous*

Three-tenths of a woman's good looks are due to nature, seven-tenths due to dress.　—*Anonymous*

Women are flowers that can talk, and flowers are women which give off a fragrance.
Rather enjoy talk than a fragrance.　—*Chang Chao*

To love a beautiful woman with the sentiment of loving flowers increases the keenness of admiration; to love flowers with the sentiment of loving women increases one's tenderness in protecting them.
—*Chang Chao*

Love, like a cough, cannot be hid.　—*Anonymous*

The young girl likes beauty; her mother likes money (in suitors).　—*Anonymous*

Man loves woman like one thirsty asking for a drink. Woman loves man like one in a hot climate seeking for a cool place. Therefore the latter stays longer.
—*Shu Shuehmou*

She who is born handsome is born with sorrow for many a man.　—*Anonymous*

BEST OF BESTSELLERS FROM
WARNER PAPERBACK LIBRARY!